Frogs and Toads

An Owner's Guide To

A HAPPY HEALTHY PET

Howell Book House

Wiley Publishing, Inc.

Howell Book House

Published by Wiley Publishing, Inc., New York, NY

For general information on our other products and services, please contact our Customer Care Department within the U.S. at 800-762-2974, outside the U.S. at 317-572-3993 or fax 317-572-4002.

Wiley also publishes its books in a variety of electronic formats. Some content that appears in print may not be available in electronic books.

Library of Congress Cataloging-in-Publication data

Grenard, Steve.
frogs and toads: an owner's guide to happy, healthy pet/by Steve Grenard.
p.cm.
Includes bibliographical references
ISBN 0-87605-444-0
1. Frogs as pets 2.Toads as Pets. 3. Frogs. 4. Toads. I. Title. II. Series.
SF459.F83G74   1998, 2001
639.3'78—dc21   97-43033
                                 CIP

Manufactured in the United States of America
10   9   8   7   6   5

Book Design: Michele Laseau
Cover Design: Michael Freeland
Photography Editor: Richard Fox
Illustration: Jeff Yesh
Photography:
   Front cover photo supplied by Chris Collins/The Stock Market
   Back cover photo supplied by William Manning/The Stock Market
   Joan Balzarini: 60
   Doug Elliot: 63
   Bill Love: 25, 35, 36–37, 38, 73, 74, 91 (bottom), 92, 98, 101, 105, 119, 120
   Zig Leszczynski: Title page, 12, 13, 21, 23, 31, 39, 41, 43, 68–69, 77, 79, 80, 81, 82, 86, 89 (bottom), 90, 91 (top), 94, 95, 96, 100, 102, 104, 106, 107, 108, 110, 111, 112, 113, 115, 116 (bottom), 117, 121
   David Schilling: 22, 116 (top)
   Mark Smith: 2–3, 11, 89 (top), 109
   Renée Stockdale: 5, 8, 9, 15, 18, 19, 27, 30, 33, 45, 49, 53, 55, 57, 66, 70, 75, 103

Contents

Frogs

and

Toads

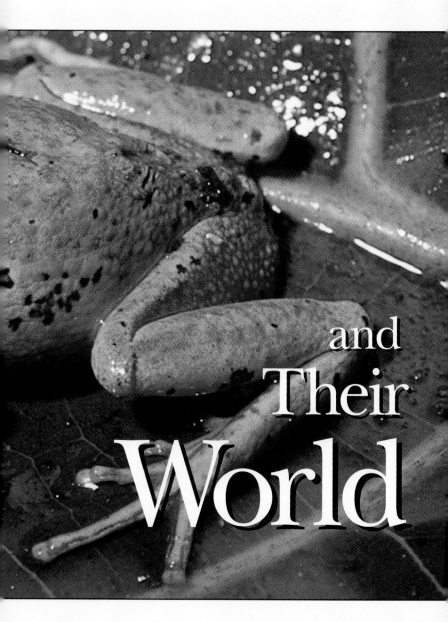

and Their World

External Features of a Typical Frog

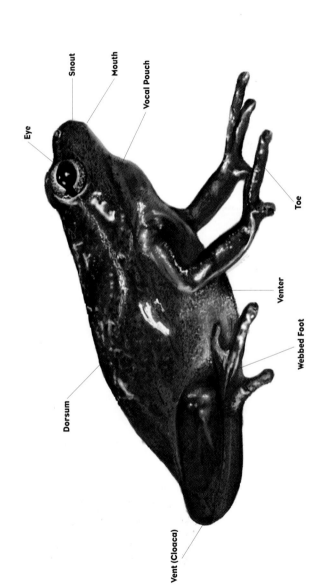

Eye

Snout

Mouth

Vocal Pouch

Toe

Venter

Dorsum

Webbed Foot

Vent (Cloaca)

chapter 1

What Are
Frogs and Toads?

Frogs and toads are four-legged, tailless, air-breathing vertebrates that represent the link between the fish and the reptiles and all other air-breathing species, including humans. Although the first amphibians, the labryinthodonts, first took the great leap from water to land during the Devonian period some 400 million years ago, fossils of frogs appear much later, in the Jurassic period of North America, some 280

million years ago. Frogs are members of a class or group of vertebrates known as the Amphibia, a word that means "dual-life" and references the fact that amphibian life history occurs in two phases—one in the water and the other on land. It also alludes to the fact that many amphibians are, well, amphibious, and are as fully at home in the water as they are on land, although there are many notable exceptions including species that never leave the water and others that stay on land or in trees and never enter the water at all. The other amphibian groups or orders include the Caudates or Urodeles, which are known familiarly as salamanders and newts, and an obscure order known as the Apoda (legless amphibians) or caecilians. These segmented, wormlike creatures are found primarily in the tropics of the world, remain burrowed in moist soil most of the time, and little is known of their habits or life history. Clearly of all the amphibians, frogs and toads are the most familiar and best studied. Frogs and toads are members of the order Anura, a term that means tailless, which is exactly what they are—bereft of a true tail, which is present in their salamander cousins.

So Many Frogs and Toads

There are more than 4,500 species of frogs and toads in the world, but nobody knows exactly how many there really are—new species and subspecies are being discovered by scientists at the rate of more than a dozen a year. Amazingly, it is predicted that such discoveries may go on indefinitely, so long as the precious habitat of these animals is protected from destruction. Environmental insults and habitat destruction has already caused the extinction of countless species over the last few decades; it is theorized that some rare species became extinct before scientists learned of their existence.

The number of different species of frogs and toads increases with warmer climates, and the neotropical and tropical regions of the world tend to have more species than the temperate or more northern, and therefore colder, climates. In one small valley (San Cecilia) in Ecuador's Amazon basin, scientists discovered a total of eighty-one species of frogs and toads, finding fifty-six in just one night! This is all the more remarkable when you consider that there are about eighty-one frog and toad species in the whole United States.

Frogs and toads are an essential part of our ecosystem. Each individual animal consumes untold quantities of insect pests in a single day and helps to keep noxious insect populations in check. Without frogs and toads, the Earth would be overrun with crop-eating and disease-spreading bugs. Their existence also provides food for larger carnivores, including humans. Their larvae, or tadpoles, consume aquatic weeds that might otherwise clog up waterways. Clearly, frogs and toads play a vital role in the environment, and there is no telling what could happen if they should suddenly all disappear, but disappearing they are. It is feared that they are declining in total number and some populations have been observed to completely vanish for no apparent reason. Even casual observers walking in wetlands they've visited for years find one spring that the frogs or toads that were once there are no longer present. More alarming still is that this loss of wildlife is occurring even in seemingly pristine and untouched habitats. These declines baffle environmentalists who hope that by studying frogs in captivity as well as in the wild they may one day solve these mysterious absences.

> ### THE GIFTS OF FROGS AND TOADS
>
> Over the centuries there have been innumerable scientific discoveries made with the assistance of these animals. They are among the first vertebrate species studied by future doctors and other scientists, and the sum total of all knowledge that people have garnered from the mere existence of frogs and toads is beyond calculation. Recently, many species have been studied as a source of valuable new drugs such as peptide antibiotics, painkillers and even anti-cancer agents. Scientists have only just touched the tip of the proverbial iceberg where this research is concerned. There is much more to learn about frogs and toads, and, if they survive, they will undoubtedly continue to confer a never-ending source of benefits to humans.

Classification of Frogs and Toads

The most basic unit of any animal or plant classification system is the species. And although there have been many efforts to try to define this word, it is impossible to establish any firm rules that apply in every case. Generally, members of a single species all look alike, live in a similar location, eat the same foods and reproduce in the same manner, usually with each other. The exception is when two different species accidentally mate and produce a hybrid. Over time, if these hybrids survive and breed with one another, a new species is eventually created.

Some animals are similar enough to be considered members of the same species but there may be slight differences in different populations. This results in a subspecies category. Above the species level, all animals that conform to each other in general appearance are members of a genus, and above that they belong to a larger group called a family.

The American Bullfrog's scientific name is Rana catesbeiana.

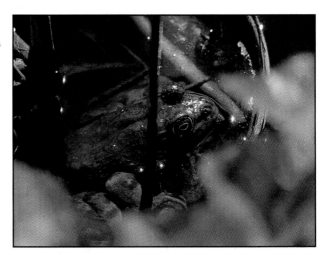

SPECIES AND SUBSPECIES

Every species has a two-part name, and subspecies have a three-part name. The first part of the name of a species is its genus and the second part is its species name. If a third part occurs, it is the subspecies designation. Thus, the American Bullfrog, with no known subspecies, is a member of the genus *Rana* and species *catesbeiana*. Its scientific name is therefore written: *Rana catesbeiana*. This frog is named after the early American naturalist Mark Catesby.

In the printed literature, Latin scientific names are always italicized. The classification of the American Bullfrog is written as follows:

Phylum	*Chordata* (animals with a spinal cord)
Sub-Phylum	*Vertebrata* (animal with a back bone or vertebral column)
Class	*Amphibia*
Family	*Ranidae*
Genus	*Rana*
Species	*catesbeiana*

There are some forty-one families of frogs and toads, but only some of the best known, most interesting and more commonly studied groups will be included, although the others will be briefly mentioned in the species accounts that follow the general information sections.

What's the Difference Between a Frog and a Toad?

The difference between a frog and a toad is actually more illusory than real. Both terms have been used interchangeably in different parts of the world. There are some generalizations that can be made specific to the American way of using the terminology. First and foremost, all toads are frogs and all frogs are also frogs. But all frogs are not necessarily toads.

This Oriental Fire Bellied Toad is, in fact, a frog.

Regardless of whether you call a particular species a toad, it is still, technically, a frog. In the United States, we tend to classify toads as mainly terrestrial or land-dwelling amphibians that enter the water only to breed and lay their eggs. We tend to think of frogs as aquatic or semi-aquatic organisms—animals that are equally at home in the water as on damp ground.

The problem with this definition is that there are frogs that never or rarely enter the water except to breed, such as the tree frogs—frogs that, as a rule, spend as much time as possible aloft in trees and about as far away from water as you can imagine. On the other hand, there are species, such as the Surinam Toad (*Pipa pipa*), that spend all of their lives in the water and would quickly die if stranded on land. In spite of its strictly aquatic lifestyle, it somehow earned the name of "toad." Therefore, all you can say about this subject is to beg the question: "What's in a name?" The only other thing one can say about the rules of giving common names to frogs and toads is that there are really no rules at all.

THE TAILLESS AMPHIBIANS

Frogs and toads are tailless amphibians and are members of the scientific order Anura. "Anura" means "tailless," a description that distinguishes frogs and toads from salamanders, the other large group of amphibians. Amphibians are believed to be the evolutionary link between fish and reptiles.

chapter 2

The Anatomy of Frogs and Toads

If you were asked how to best describe the average frog or toad, you would have to say that they have relatively broad bodies (although a few types are slimmer), no identifiable neck, no tail and four legs. The rear legs are one and one-half to three times longer than the front legs. The mouth is

broad and sits below the snout at the front of the body, whereas the other end of the gastrointestinal tract terminates in a structure known as the cloaca, through which both liquid and solid wastes pass, as well as eggs in females and sperm cells in males. The eyes are prominent orbs that sit at the top of the head. The frog skeleton looks very similar from one species to the next, although a trained eye can discern differences between various species.

*The African
Snake-Necked
Frog can turn its
head from side
to side.*

Frogs and toads are ectotherms, which means that they cannot produce their own internal body heat. Thus, they are constantly moving about, either to cool off or warm up.

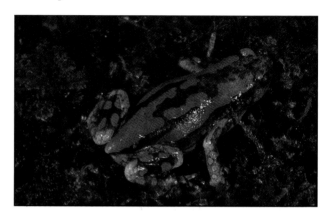

Limbs and Locomotion

Although frogs descended from their tailed predecessors, the salamanders, which wattle or scuttle along using all four legs in some sort of a rhythmic but seemingly discordant fashion, frogs and toads improved on this form of locomotion by developing the ability to jump or, at worst, hop along at speeds that far exceed that of any terrestrial salamander. Some larger species can jump prodigious distances. In fact, some frogs can jump so fast and so far they have earned themselves the common name of rocket frogs, and there are so many fantastic leapers among the frogs it is difficult to decide which species outshine others. In general, the Ranid or water frogs, such as the American Bullfrog and its relative the African Giant Bullfrog (*Conraua goliath*), are the species most often entered into frog-jumping contests. When it comes to getting around, the remarkable Flying Frogs of the genus *Rhacophorus* can actually glide from branch to

> **NOT ALL FROGS ARE NECKLESS**
>
> Although one would have a tough time locating the neck on most frogs, one group of five African frogs are an interesting exception to this rule. The Snake-Necked Frogs (*Phrynomantis sp.*) have a clearly discernible neck that they can even turn side to side. This ability may not sound too impressive to us, but to a frog, this is quite a feat!

branch, holding onto branches with specially modified fingertips.

Although large Ranids such as the African Giant Bullfrog or Goliath Frog are prodigious jumpers, a frog's size is not often a factor in its ability to jump long distances. The tiny Black-Spotted Tree Frog (*Hyla nigromaculata*), which measures a scant 1.2 inches from the tip of its nose to its cloacal vent, can jump a distance of nearly 5 feet! And the smallish Carpathian Frog (*Rana dalmatina*) has been recorded jumping over 9 feet.

The slowest and clumsiest of frogs and toads is open to debate. Some would argue that the large, heavy land toads (of the genus *Bufo*) that hop around in short bursts are the winners in these categories. Others would contend that the frogs known commonly as Walking Frogs, which are capable of getting around only by walking slowly and deliberately toward their objective, have the least impressive gait. These frogs are condemned to walking as a result of their poorly developed, though quite normal, hind limb musculature. Similarly, the Narrow-mouthed Toads (*Breviceps sp.*) crawl or creep around (at best).

The African Giant Bullfrog is known for its ability to jump long distances.

Frog and Toad "Fingers"

At least two species of frogs, the species *Chiroleptes platicephalus* and the tree frogs of the genus *Phyllomedusa,* possess an opposable thumb. Frogs and toads have four fingers or front limb digits and five hind limb digits or toes. In aquatic and semiaquatic species there may be either slight or extensive webbing between the toes to facilitate swimming. Nails or claws are unknown in frogs and toads with three exceptions: the African

Clawed Frogs (*Xenopus sp.* and *Silurana sp.*) and a burrowing species of toad known as *Rhinophrynus dorsalis*. The fingertips of these species have keratinized or thickened coverings resembling nails or claws.

SWIMMING

Most frogs are excellent swimmers. To propel themselves in the water, they use their hind legs exclusively, keeping their front limbs pressed against their sides. Aquatic and semiaquatic species have webbed hind feet, which increase surface contact with the water and accelerate propulsion. The webbed feet of frogs served as inspiration for the flippers used by divers—who, during World War II, were nicknamed "frogmen" as a testament to the animals that taught them how to swim efficiently underwater.

Frog Senses

Frogs and toads have the same sort of senses as other animals and people do: vision, taste, smell, hearing and touch. In addition, their larvae or tadpoles and some fully aquatic adult species have a lateral line system responsible for special senses needed for moving about underwater.

THE SIXTH SENSE: LATERAL LINE ORGANS

Scientists believe that the lateral line organs or systems exist as a special sixth sense to let their owners sense water temperature conditions, water currents and the existence of bioelectrical fields. Both marine and freshwater fish can detect galvanic signals (electric currents in the water) via their lateral line systems, although this ability is not proven in frogs and toads. The lateral line systems occur in almost all frog and toad tadpoles but disappear at metamorphosis. The strictly aquatic frogs, such as *Xenopus sp.* and *Pipa sp.,* retain a lateral line organ system into adulthood and it is believed to enable these animals to locate mobile objects moving through the water in their vicinity. Because these frogs have small, practically useless eyes, this is an important compensatory sense that helps them navigate underwater.

Vision

The eyes of frogs come in every conceivable color and pupil shape (round, vertical, horizontal, diamond-shaped), and they are one of the most unique and beautiful attributes of many species. The eyes of some species blend with facial and body coloration and patterns to make them a more difficult target for an attacker.

Bufonid toads have eyes that are flecked with gold and black; others are black with flecks of red or oange pigments. Species with blue, green and silver and gold eyes exist as well. Most frogs have a mirrorlike layer (known as the *tapetum lucidium*) in the rear of their

Frogs' eyes are located on the top and side of the head. (White's Tree Frog)

eyes that enables them to reflect light at night—an attribute known as "eye-shine." If you cast a bright searchlight around an area populated by frogs, their eye-shine will stand out above anything else in the pitch blackness of night.

The eyes of frogs are located in eye sockets mounted atop and on each side of the head. Frogs can see sideways and partially rearward (independently to the left and right with each eye). However, they have only a 40- to 60-degree overlap frontwards, which gives them limited binocular vision. Frogs use their eyesight to espy the smallest movement of a possible prey item, and for this reason they are extremely farsighted—easily seeing objects 50 feet away but unable to discern anything right under their nose. It is, in fact, their olfactory sense that they use when a prey item is just about on top of them. It has been noted that the eyes retract down into their sockets when a frog or toad swallows its prey and the pressure exerted by the eyes during swallowing aids ingestion as a result.

Underwater Vision

Frogs have movable eyelids and, in addition, a semitrans-parent, somewhat opaque, membranous eye cover called the nictitating membrane. This membrane protects the eyes when they need to be open underwater. Vision, however, is clearly limited and swimming frogs can probably only see shadows underwater in contrast to any acute sense of vision that they have to see on land. Underwater, frogs are more likely to detect an object through their olfactory sense rather than through their vision.

FROGS CAN (ALMOST) SEE IN COLOR

Frogs have some limited degree of color vision that favors the blue/green end of the spectrum. This is believed to be an adaptation that aids them when they need to escape and do so by leaping into the water, which is also at the blue end of the spectrum in terms of its reflected light. "Head for the blue . . ." would be the warning cry of frogs in danger—or, on the other hand, if they were tree frogs, it would be "head for the green . . . "

HEARING

Frogs have an elaborate repertoire of vocalizations or calls that serve a variety of purposes, ranging from advertising for a mate to alerting others to danger (see "Frog Communications" later in this chapter). Their voice would be of little use unless they had a first-class listening system to go along with it. All frogs and toads (with the exception of species in the genus *Bombina,* such as the Oriental Fire Bellied Toads) have a prominent external eardrum or tympanum located slightly above and to the rear of their eyes. They have no outer ear, although a few species have the vestiges of an outer earlobe or shell that serves to protect the eardrum as well as direct the sound. Although the tympanum is prominent and easy to spot in large species like the American Bullfrog and its relatives, in others it is well disguised and sports the coloration of the head and body, making it difficult to see. Sounds reaching the eardrum are conducted directly to the hearing structures located internally in back of it.

Frogs do not use their hearing to locate prey or sense danger. In one experiment, a chorus of calling frogs sitting in shallow water were subjected to the loud bang of a firecracker beyond their line of vision. They were unperturbed and continued to sing. On the other hand, a potential enemy that came into their line of sight caused them to retreat—as did the vibrations made on the surface of the water by slapping it with a canoe paddle. And while a warning or distress call uttered by a frog in imminent danger may cause all the other frogs in the area to go on red alert, it seems to take a lot more to elicit any activity from them. Frogs, therefore, seem to best use their hearing for making love (not war) and rely more heavily on visual, tactile and olfactory senses for feeding and threat detection.

SMELL

Frogs and toads unquestionably have a keen sense of smell that receives olfactory stimuli from at least two different sets of receptor organs—the conventional nasal passages and their Jacobson's organ located in the roof of their mouths. When a frog or toad picks up the scent of food, it is stimulated to search for it as the odor stimulus does not seem to pinpoint location so much as it merely indicates presence in the general vicinity. The stronger the odor of a familiar substance, the greater the excitement level will be—whether odor detection of a predator, which dictates escape, or the sweet smell of a meal, which promotes frantic searching.

On detecting the odor of food, frogs will face in the general direction of the smell and begin to make grasping and mouth-opening movements, not realizing that the object of their desire may still be somewhat far off. When the food item comes within about $\frac{1}{2}$ inch or less of the frog, its olfactory senses tell it that the meal is at hand. Frogs and toads in the water may also perceive a warning odor, an odorous stimulus liberated by a wounded frog, toad or tadpole nearby. It signals the unscathed frogs that a predator is around and that they should retreat.

Although calling is the primary means by which frogs and toads find their mates, it is likely that odor and marking of territory play some role in this activity. Odor detection is also used for navigating and spatial orientation. Frogs, given the choice of running a T-shaped maze with pure, distilled (no odor) water on one side and natural pond water on the other, invariably head for the pond water. Other species have been conditioned to associate odors with various objectives in maze experiments, and such conditioning based on odors works extremely well. Some toads have learned to discriminate among a wide range of odoriferous substances, including cedar balsam, creosote and geranium oil. It is also possible to confound the olfactory senses of frogs. In experiments with flies (which they love to eat) and a type of bug that they loathe, it was possible to confuse the frogs so badly that they ignored the flies when they should have been gobbling them up.

Frogs have a keen sense of smell. (White's Tree Frog)

TASTE

Frogs and toads, while they are less than discriminatory in what they will eat, do actively use their sense of taste to reject bugs and other prey items that do not taste just right to them. The taste buds are embedded in the epithelium of the tongue and in the mucous membranes of the oral cavity. They sense the four basic taste categories: sweet, bitter, sour and salty. Their sense of taste helps them to reject unwanted vegetable matter swept up in a feeding frenzy, as well as to reject insects that may be poisonous to them if fully ingested. Frogs and toads will disgorge intended food matter that they find unpalatable without regard for table manners. They will even use their front legs to remove such items.

Touch

Frogs and toads appear readily sensitive to heat, cold, rough and smooth surfaces, as well as to pain. Their sense of touch helps them to avoid potentially harmful situ-ations, and of all their sensory input, it is the most intimate, up close and directly transmitted of the senses.

Frog Skin

Not all frogs and toads are green, contrary to what most children brought up on heavy doses of Kermit and other cartoonish frog characters are led to believe. In fact, frogs and toads run the gamut from the common green color to browns, grays and bright, garish colors like red, yellow and bright blue. It is safe to say that somewhere, someplace, there is a frog with just about any color and pattern you can imagine.

Frogs need to keep their skin moist. (White's Tree Frog)

The Colorful Frog

Frogs that tend to be colored in the greenish, brown and gray ends of the color scale use their coloration for "crypsis" or blending in with their surroundings. Frog skin designed to disguise them helps prevent frogs from being eaten by predators. It also allows frogs to remain unseen as a prey item wanders into range. Bright colors such as reds and yellows are known as "warning colors." Species with these colors are advertising to potential predators that they are dangerous to eat because of poisonous secretions.

19

SENSITIVE SKIN

Unlike fish, reptiles, birds and mammals, amphibian skin has no scales, feathers or hair to protect it; this makes amphibians unique. All of their skin must be kept moist to facilitate cutaneous respiration and water absorption—the only real exception being the back in rough-skinned, leathery toads. In addition, many species have skin heavily endowed with glands that produce both a protective layer of mucouslike material as well as a variety of proteins, alkaloids and other poisonous or antibiotic substances.

Their mucous coat helps protect frogs from drying out or dehydrating, and their noxious secretions cause many predators to drop a frog or toad once they get a taste of such substances. Many predators are not likely to forget such an experience and tend to steer clear from ever trying to eat a frog or toad again, especially those that sport warning colors mentioned above.

MOLTING

Like all species, frogs shed or molt their skin—some as often as daily. They do this by starting to eat it where it ends around their mouth. Other species will dislodge pieces of their membranous epidermal layer, and you will find it floating around in their water bowl, lying in the corners of their enclosures or smeared onto the glass walls of their aquariums. Remove all dead skin by netting it up and flushing it in the toilet. Discarding uneaten pieces of molted skin is an important part of keeping your frog or toad's home hygienic, as the dead skin can provide an ideal medium and surface area for the culture of fungi and bacteria.

Frog Communications

Frogs are the only amphibians with a true voice, although salamanders have been heard to make clicking sounds. Frog calls are famous for their variety, resonance and resemblance to other sounds. The call of the Common American Green Frog (*Rana clamitans*), for example, sounds like someone strumming on a banjo! When frogs call in unison this is called a chorus, and such night sounds are a cardinal sign that life still exists in the darkness long after others have gone to sleep.

Frogs have a variety of different calls, and no two species of frog have the same call or call on the same sound frequency. Calls are used by both males and females, although the loudest calls are made by the males when seeking a mate—an advertising call. Males who are mated by other males will emit a special call known as a release call, telling the amorous suitor, in effect, to get lost. And if one frog gets in trouble or is attacked, it will emit a distress call, warning all frog brethren in the area that something bad is going down. There are even frogs that can call underwater!

The Common American Green Frog calling.

Frog call recordings are available and many scientists spend their careers studying these calls, their sound frequencies and significance. The U.S. National Biological Survey uses the distinctive call of frogs to determine whether or not a particular species still lives in areas where it existed previously, and the deafening call of some French frogs is alleged to have been the final straw causing the outbreak of the French Revolution in 1789. According to this folk tale, the French nobility were being kept awake by the frogs on July 12, 1789. The next evening, they ordered their servants to stay up all night and whenever the servants heard the frogs start to call, they were to slap the water with sticks and paddles to shut them up. This degrading request was the ultimate insult to be heaved upon the peasants, and the next day, July 14th, they stormed the Bastille! Whether this story is true or not is a matter of conjecture but the timing is right: In France, the first two weeks of July are prime frog-calling time.

21

Frogs and Toads in the Wild

Frogs and toads inhabit virtually every habitat the earth has to offer—from surface terrain to trees to caves to subterranean burrows that they excavate themselves with specialized feet. They also live in and around ponds, creeks, streams, lakes, swamps and rivers—any imaginable freshwater body of water, including those that are man-made. Frogs and toads can be found miles up on mountains as well as below sea level in valleys and river basins. They occupy jungles, forests, plains, tundra, scrubland and deserts, but no frog or toad can tolerate full-strength seawater due to their permeable skin. Contact with saltwater would quickly poison them, as, unlike reptiles and many marine species, they have no means of excreting excess salt. A few species are found in brackish or estuarine habitats. These include the Marine or Giant Tropical Toad (*Bufo marinus*) and the European Natterjack Toad (*Bufo calamita*). There is, however, no need to duplicate such habitats for these species in captivity. Their presence in brackish or low-salinity environments is an aberration that they can tolerate but which they definitely do not require.

Releasing Frogs and Toads into the Wild

In a word, "Don't." Allowing captive frogs or toads to escape into the wild or deliberately releasing them is an irresponsible act that could conceivably have dire consequences for the environment and for other wild frogs and toads. Never consider releasing any non-native species into a new habitat. If that species should happen to prosper, it could compete with, crowd out

Dart-poison frogs from South America have been introduced into Hawaii. (Blue Dart-Poison Frog)

or quite possibly even eat other frogs, toads and species it was not intended to harm. There are many examples of the havoc caused by such releases or escapes throughout the world. The American Bullfrog, for example, uses up natural resources intended for other animals worldwide, including some in the United States.

Another giant species, the Marine Toad, has caused similar problems. It was deliberately released on many islands including Hawaii and Australia. It is a tough species, reproduces at enormous rates and has established itself at the expense of native species, which in many places it gobbles up with abandon. The overabundance of African Clawed Frogs in California waters is yet another example.

South American Dart-Poison Frogs, Cuban Tree Frogs, Japanese Wrinkled Frogs and American Bullfrogs all have been deliberately or accidentally introduced into Hawaii. The Bullfrog has even earned itself a Hawaiian name: *poloka lana*. The Cuban Tree Frog, which found its way to south Florida, can now be found throughout the southern half of the state, and native tree frogs have either died out or have become extremely scarce.

And if you ever contemplate rereleasing a native frog back into its own habitat, it is wise to reconsider. In captivity, frogs and toads may pick up and become immune to bacteria and viruses that wild living frogs and toads have never encountered. It is conceivable that a germ introduced by a released captive could eradicate an entire population of wild frogs. In fact, infectious diseases may well be responsible for some notable frog disappearances. There is no use tempting fate by such well-intentioned but misguided actions. If you can no longer keep a frog or toad, give it away—back to the pet shop, a local school, a zoo or a friend. If you try, you will find someone who wants your unwanted frog.

The above admonition notwithstanding, release of captive-bred species back into their natural or native habitat is done occasionally to repopulate areas where such species once existed but have disappeared. Such release programs, however, are done under the strictest scientific and veterinary medical scrutiny. Professional biologists, veterinarians, conservationists, environmental scientists and fish and game professionals are all consulted in such planned events. An individual who thinks that he can engage in such a program on his own is simply courting disaster.

Water and Electrolyte Balance

Frogs and toads have a thin, membranelike permeable skin over all or most parts of their bodies. As a result, they rapidly absorb and excrete water and its constituents between their bodies and their environment. This includes electrolytes in the form of mineral salts dissolved in their watery environment. Water supplied to captive frogs and toads should *always* be fresh water, treated to remove chlorine and to maintain normal pH for the species involved. Because frogs rapidly foul their captive aquatic environment, water should be vigorously filtered and/or changed frequently to remove noxious organic waste matter.

American Spadefoot Toads emerge from the soil when they hear rain falling.

Frogs and toads also exchange gases (oxygen and carbon dioxide) through their skin, and so they must keep all or a good part of their skin moist at all times. Even thick or leathery skinned Bufonid toads have thinner skin on their underbellies and the undersides of their legs and rump, and they exchange water, electrolytes and gases through regions in contact with the substrate that they are occupying. Frogs and many toads are constantly in danger of dehydrating and dying if insufficient or no water is present in their environment, although a few species have adapted to arid desertlike conditions by digging well into the substrate to find moisture and remaining below until conditions at the surface improve. The American Spadefoot Toads (*Scaphiopus sp.*) know to dig their way out of their self-imposed subterranean cocoons when they hear raindrops hitting the surface above them. They rapidly do so, breed and lay their eggs in temporary ponds or puddles. Their eggs and larvae develop quickly in such temporary bodies of water, and then the newly transformed frogs take a few meals and dig in again to await the next cycle of rain. Such species also develop extra

25

layers of skin to prevent drying out even if subterranean conditions become drier than usual. They can also tolerate dehydration to a far greater degree than other species. Spadefoot Toads are estimated to be able to lose up to half of their total body weight in water without harm.

Temperature Regulation

Frogs and toads, like reptiles, fish and all other amphibians, are ectothermic—a term that means they derive their body temperature from the temperature around them. Unlike birds and mammals, which produce their own heat metabolically in spite of external temperature, frogs and toads are completely dependent on their environment in this respect. This has important implications for anyone keeping frogs or toads in a captive or unnatural environment. It is necessary under such circumstances to make sure you duplicate external temperature and temperature variations as closely as possible to a particular species' natural environment. You can easily overheat a frog or toad with the result that it would stop feeding, reduce or curtail its natural activity levels and, in some extremes, quickly die as a result. In nature, ectotherms regulate their body temperature by constantly moving from warmer to cooler spots, from sunny to shady areas, by burrowing into the substrate or diving into the water or emerging from it. Generally, most amphibians prefer temperatures on the cooler side, as excessive warmth enhances the potential for evaporative dehydration. Tropical species used to warmer temperatures must also be kept in containers with a high relative humidity. Dry heat under any circumstances is dangerous to just about all amphibians. In addition to changing their environment, frogs also regulate their temperature by changing their skin color—lightening up to deflect heat and darkening to absorb it.

Hibernation and Estivation

When conditions at the surface become either too hot or too cold, frogs that live in areas of climatic extremes cannot migrate to more hospitable environments as fish, birds and some mammals do. Instead they resort to one of two things: They either hibernate to escape the extreme cold or estivate to escape excessive heat. When temperatures start to drop, frog activity levels begin to drop along with it. They pass their last meal and eat no more, their heart and respirations slow and they become more and more lethargic until they move no more. Although a scant few species can survive total freezing thanks to their ability to manufacture a glycerol-based cellular antifreeze, most frogs and toads either dig into the substrate, whether it's at the bottom of a pond or on the forest floor, to levels just below the eventual frostline and wait for favorable conditions to return at the surface.

Hibernation Practices Vary

The most cold-tolerant species of frog reside in North America. The Wood Frog (*Rana sylvatica*), the Spring Peeper (*Pseudacris crucifer*), the Gray Tree Frog (*Hyla versicolor*) and the Boreal Toad (*Bufo boreas*) emerge from hibernation months before other species, even while

The Gray Tree Frog tolerates cold well—it lives in northern Canada.

there still may be snow on the ground. The Gray Tree Frog extends well into Manitoba, Canada; the Wood Frog as far north as the Yukon and North-west Territories and the Alaskan tundra, just inside the Arctic Circle. Spring Peepers and Boreal Toads extend far north into Canada as well. These "freeze-tolerant" species are able to manufacture excessive amounts of glycerol, which serves as a cellular antifreeze

of sorts and prevents cells from freezing completely under the coldest conditions. While freezing of cells is not a problem, the cells often rupture when thawing out and this is what causes the death of an organism that becomes frozen alive. These species survive months of freezing with about sixty-five percent of their total body water as ice and have been found encased in blocks of ice, only to be slowly thawed and fully recovered.

ESTIVATING SPECIES

Obviously, neotropical and tropical species from the American south to the equator do not hibernate, but these species practice another sort of inactivity to prevent their metabolic collapse during periods of excessive climatic heat—they dig in to the cooler substrate or damp earth and estivate. Frogs and toads also estivate during periods of excessive dryness to conserve precious body water until the rain reappears. Among the species that do this regularly are many desert and plains species such as the American Spadefoot Toads (*Scaphiopus sp.*) and the Australian Water-Holding Frogs (*Cyclorana sp.*). The biology of hibernation—lowered metabolism, diminished circulation and a curtailed need for oxygen and carbon dioxide elimination via breathing during extreme cold is fairly well understood; the means by which frogs do this under conditions of extreme heat and aridity is not as well documented.

Frog and Toad Size and Growth Patterns

The largest frog in the world is the West African (Goliath) Bullfrog, *Conraua goliath,* which, when measured from the tip of its snout to its cloacal vent (a standardized measure known as snout-vent or s-v length), can reach a foot or more in length. Other large frogs include the Giant Tropical or Marine/Cane Toad (*Bufo marinus*), the Colorado River Toad (*Bufo alvarius*), the South American Blomberg's Toad (*Bufo blombergi*) and the American Bullfrog (*Rana catesbeiana*). Male African Bullfrogs (*Pyxicephalus adpersus*) can reach snout-vent lengths of 10 inches. They are often nicknamed "pyxie" frogs because of their scientific name but this has nothing to do with their eventual size. The other giants of the frog world also grow up to 8 to 10 inches s-v length.

However, most frogs and toads reach nowhere near these sizes and range from miniature species of less than ¼ inch to mid-range sizes of 4 to 6 inches.

From Tadpole to Adult

An interesting paradox about frog and toad tadpoles is that as they develop into fully formed frogs they actually grow shorter instead of longer. This is because frog and toad larvae or tadpoles have tails that disappear as they grow into fully formed four-legged adults. Thus a 2-inch tadpole, when it finishes transforming into a baby froglet, may be only ½ inch in s-v length. The frog then starts to grow again, only this time it is its body that becomes longer and larger. The Paradoxical Frog got its name for just this reason—this species begins life as a particularly large tadpole that metamorphoses into a particularly tiny froglet.

The amount of time it takes a frog or toad egg to transform into a tadpole and a tadpole into a fully formed froglet or toadlet depends on the species as well as a variety of external factors including water conditions, temperature and availability of food. Some species born into temporary pools, even puddles or rain deposits in the cup of leaves metamorphose quite rapidly. If they didn't, they would be doomed to die without developing into an air-breathing land, aquatic or semiaquatic adult. Thus it can take anywhere from a few weeks to two or three months for some species to metamorphose.

> ### THE UNIQUE AMERICAN TAILED FROG
>
> The American Tailed Frog is special in several ways. Nearly one-third of the tadpole body length consists of its mouth, not counting the tail. Its mouth is huge, rounded and looks and works like a vacuum cleaner. What's more, adult Tailed Frogs have no lungs and breathe only through the skin. Their lack of lungs also means that they have no voice; so, unlike most frogs, they have to find other ways to locate mates. It is theorized that they sniff out potential mates using pheromones.

Reproduction in Frogs and Toads

There is no more fascinating aspect of frog and toad study than the means by which they mate, breed, lay their eggs and develop their larvae or tadpoles. The study of frog and toad reproduction is characterized by one word: "exceptions." No single order or group of related animals, in which the majority conform to a fairly uniform means of reproduction, have as many different reproductive processes as the frogs and toads. They are utterly and without a single doubt the most fascinating and most diverse group of animals when it comes to mating, reproduction and life history.

A 2-inch tadpole will develop into a froglet of ½ inch in length.

THE STANDARD REPRODUCTIVE PROCESS

It is hard for anyone familiar with all these exceptions to believe that there is a norm or standard; however, some reproductive "rules" do prevail. The vast majority of female frogs find mates by answering the mating calls of the males during the breeding season. When a mating occurs, usually in the water, the male grasps the female by placing his front legs either around her waist or around her chest under her front legs. This grasp is known as *amplexsus*. He then proceeds to squeeze the unfertilized eggs out of the female, depositing sperm and fertilizing them all at once. The eggs then develop in the water, either floating in strings or clumps, or attaching themselves to pieces of vegetation or rock formations.

The unicellular egg starts dividing and it soon becomes a multicellular sphere transforming itself into a tadpole or larva. Now begins the second stage of a frog or toad's development. The tadpoles are strictly aquatic organisms and, as a rule, develop in the water.

Tadpoles eat either vegetable matter, animal matter or a combination of both, and many species of tadpole are cannibalistic as well. The tadpole starts to sprout legs, first the front legs and then the hind legs. At the same time, its long tail is reabsorbed and disappears and its gills are lost in favor of lungs—although all frogs and toads can also breathe through their skin. Many species still retain some vestiges of their tail as they emerge onto land but this is quickly lost. This process is known as *metamorphosis,* a word that literally means structural change. At this point, the newly minted froglets or toadlets, as the case may be, emerge from the water and are ready to lead an amphibious existence, on land and in the water.

EXCEPTIONS TO THE RULES

As noted earlier, there are many exceptions to the "standard" processes. First, there are the frogs that deposit their eggs in the water. For the vast majority of frogs and toads, this can be either permanent or tem-

A Wood Frog tad-pole transforming into a baby frog.

porary, standing or even running water. But then there are frog moms who deposit their eggs in natural or specially constructed basins of water. There are tree frogs that deposit their eggs in the cups of leaves or aerial plants and others that use standing water accumulated in tree holes. The Strawberry Dart-Poison Frog (*Dendorbate pumilio*) first lays five to ten eggs on a horizontal leaf; both the male and female visit them regularly and keep them moist by urinating on them. When they become tadpoles, the female carries each one to its own individual water bath fash-ioned out of the deep leaves of nearby aerial plants. She places a single egg in the cup of a bromeliad or epiphyte plant and returns to each tadpole and deposits several nonfertile eggs for the tadpole to feed on. This is but one of the most remarkable discoveries in the fascinating world of frog and toad behaviors, and no one could believe that these lowly animals confer this kind of parental care on their offspring when it was first observed in a greenhouse population of these frogs.

Another unusual reproductive activity was engaged in by the Australian Gastric Brooding Frog (*Rheobatrachus silus*). This species was discovered just before it became extinct. This remarkable frog, and a close relative now also thought to be extinct, laid its eggs in the water where they were fertilized and then swallowed by the female. The eggs and tadpoles complete their development in the stomach, and the baby froglets emerged from the mother's mouth some time later. The biochemical means this species used to turn its stomach into a womb will probably never be known.

There are also species that deposit their eggs in foam nests they build on or near ponds and streams without actually entering the water. And then there is the Surinam Toad, a strictly aquatic frog that incubates its eggs under a sheath of epithelial tissue on its back. There are yet other species that deposit their eggs on damp ground (sometimes in excavated nests). The eggs are left at a specific time, so that they will develop into aquatic larvae in time for flooding, when they will be carried into the water in runoff. When the flooding does not occur as anticipated, some species carry the tadpoles to the water themselves by allowing them to wriggle up onto their legs and back. The South American Marsupial Frogs, a large group of tree frogs (*Gastrotheca sp.*), have a pouch. After fertilization, the female carries the eggs in the pouch where they develop either into free-living tadpoles or fully formed frogs. When they are ready to be liberated, the female stretches open the pouch with her hind legs allowing her babies to drop out. The male Darwin's Frog (*Rhinoderma darwini*) carries the eggs in its vocal pouch and the male of the European Midwife Toad (*Alytes obstetricians*) also gets into the act by carrying the eggs on its hind legs until they develop.

Frogs, Toads and the Law

In many states, some species of frogs are protected as endangered species. Where they are not endangered, they are still subject to hunting and fishing regulations that prohibit their collection during certain times of the year, and they are also subject to bag and size limits in many jurisdictions. Strangely, a lot of states classify frogs as fish for the purpose of game regulation (this has probably occurred just for the sake of expediency), and while this is clearly scientifically inaccurate, it helps to benefit frogs in the same way fishing regulations protect fish stocks. Therefore, before one goes out and collects some local frogs for pet purposes it is a good idea to check with local regulations first to avoid the possibility of receiving a fine and summons to appear in court. Frog-lovers are, however, incensed by the callousness of states categorizing frogs as mere fish and are lobbying for changes so that their special status can be appreciated.

African Clawed Frogs are banned in California (albino).

There are no known local laws in the U.S. that prohibit the keeping of frogs in general, but there are some specific exceptions. The highly aquatic African Clawed Frog, for example, is banned in the state of California. This popular aquarium pet and laboratory frog has been accidentally released in some California waters where it has established reproducing populations that concern California environmentalists. These frogs are not traditional members of the state's ecosystem and they are harming native species either by competing with them or by eating them. Before the situation grew any worse, California took the step of banning these frogs from the state except by special permit, and such permits are only granted to legitimate medical and scientific

33

research facilities. African Clawed Frogs in California are treated like a deadly plague virus and are subject to strict controls where their licensed use is involved.

In addition to the federal Endangered Species Act, which protects primarily U.S. species, by far the most wide-sweeping international regulation of rare, endangered and threatened populations of frogs, is the Convention on Trade in Endangered Species, or CITES for short. This is a United Nations sponsored organization of which many of the most important consumer nations are signatories, including the U.S. Thus, if a species of frog from India, for example, is on the Convention's endangered species list, it cannot be imported into the U.S. without CITES documents detailing everything about the animal. CITES is a permit system of sorts, but it is really a means by which trade is tracked and, if necessary, checked.

In cases where a shipment is suspect or the species is severely endangered, the CITES authority is likely to refuse documentation of the shipment. If it is shipped in anyway, the United States considers it smuggled contraband and will confiscate the animals, arrest the consignees inside the U.S. and prosecute them and the shippers (if possible) for criminal violations. Other nation signatories that catch smugglers inside their borders will also prosecute them for violation of the international treaty that they have agreed to honor. A domestic U.S. law known as the Lacy Act makes it a federal crime to cause the interstate transport of an endangered species without a special permit from the U.S. Department of the Interior. This law also applies to the movement of any animal or plant that is moved from a state where its possession may be legal to one where it is not legal, and it is triggered at U.S. borders where foreign endangered or illegal species are concerned as well.

Because the U.S. and international list of endangered, threatened or species of special concern changes so rapidly, readers with Internet access can go to the World Wide Web for information on both

U.S. and foreign species by logging onto: http://www. xmission.com/~gastown/herpmed/allherp.htm, which covers conservation and herpetology law, and from there click on either the United States Fish and Wildlife Service link or the link for the World Conservation Monitoring Center/CITES, as well as various state links for the latest information.

It is only recently that environmental scientists have discovered that our frog friends are in peril and their numbers are dwindling or disappearing completely. In just ten years, Australian Gastric Brooding Frogs and the spectacular Costa Rican Golden Toad have become extinct for no readily apparent reason, although everything from the hole in the ozone layer (causing excessive UV radiation) to acid rain has been implicated. Among the U.S. species in serious trouble are the Houston Toad, the Puerto Rican Crested Toad, the Colorado River Toad, the Cascades Frog, the Tailed Frog and the Western Spadefoot Toad. Even one of America's most common species, the ubiquitous Leopard Frog (*Rana pipiens*) is imperiled in many locations.

The Colorado River Toad is facing trouble as a species.

Many scientists consider amphibians as sentinel species—proverbial miners' canaries whose problems foretell greater uncertainties for people. They blame man for destroying frog habitats with toxic waste, garbage and sewage, heavy metal residues, radioactive wastes, pesticides, herbicides and chemical fertilizers. Sadly, greater-than-normal numbers of deformed and multiple-limbed abnormal frogs are being discovered in the wild. No one is quite sure of the causes of these deformities or if they are even a part of the declining frog problem. But while the debate rages on, frogs continue to disappear. Kermit the Frog in the book *One Frog Can Make a Difference* probably said it best: "If you wait until the frogs and toads have croaked their last to take some action, you've missed the point."

Living
with

part two

Frogs
and
Toads

chapter 4

Choosing
a Frog
or Toad

A number of issues should dictate your choice of a first frog or toad. Your experience level with these types of pets is an important factor. It pays to start out with inexpensive, common species, and once you succeed with these for a year or more, it may be time to move on to rarer, prettier, more exotic and more expensive frogs.

Here in the U.S. you can readily find American Bullfrogs, Leopard Frogs, Green Frogs and a variety of common toads for sale in pet shops. A few more expensive and exotic species are not much more difficult to maintain than these common Aerican species, however. The South American Horned Frogs (*Ceratophrys sp.*) need little space in spite of their large size and will eat just about anything (graduating to small mice as they get larger). They move little and are content to sit and await prey. They have an amazingly beautiful mosaic coloration of green, gold, brown and black. These frogs are considerably more costly than common U.S. species, but are being bred in captivity. Even albinos are being bred and their price is bound to drop as they become more plentiful. Regardless of what frog you choose, make sure that its holding tank at the pet shop or other animal dealer is clean, that the animal's skin is normally colored (not dark or not light) and that it does not show any obvious signs of deformity. Once you definitely decide you are going to buy the frog chosen, you should ask for one final test—to see it eat. If the dealer has no food to feed it or otherwise refuses, you might think twice about how this frog was being maintained until now. If the frog does not eat or shows difficulty in eating, this may indicate that the frog has a serious problem that you don't want to inherit. If you cannot find interesting frogs for your collection locally, you can buy them by mail order. Tracking down breeders and importers of interesting frogs can be done by reading the popular magazines that deal with reptiles and amphibians and contacting their advertisers. These publications, as well as groups involved in frog husbandry, are listed in chapter 9. Another means of acquiring frogs and toads is to attend swap meets, which are held all over the U.S. and overseas on a regular basis. There are always a few frog and toad sellers there among the more popular reptile dealers.

Before you purchase a frog, ask to see it eat. Here, a Gray Tree Frog enjoys a cricket.

Before buying your frog, make sure that you are ready for it the minute you bring it through your door. A checklist may help:

❑ Housing setup ready and waiting. Include lighting, temperature, humidity and rainmaking or misting equipment. In a pinch a plant mister bottle can be used manually in lieu of automated equipment.

❑ Handling and first aid equipment in place.

❑ A small supply of live food at hand and a reliable steady source established in advance.

❑ A few gallon jugs of aged, chlorine-free tap water or natural spring water.

LOOK FOR THESE QUALITIES WHEN CHOOSING A FROG OR TOAD

1. good appetite

2. eyes open and alert

3. normal coloration (not too dark and not too light)

4. appropriate skin texture

5. hops when gently prodded

6. normal hopping and leaping

7. plump and hearty in appearance

This slim volume is by no means the end-all of everything you will ever learn about frogs, so you may want to locate and purchase additional books on frogs and toads in general as well as material on the frog or toad that you own. You can find lists of such books by searching the World Wide Web or by requesting price lists and catalogs from specialized herpetology book dealers that advertise in various amphibian and reptile magazines.

chapter 5

Feeding
Your Frog
or Toad

When describing the food and
feeding habits of any animal,
it is helpful to know the lan-
guage used to characterize
these habits. Carnivorous animals are eaters of animal pro-
tein, including insects; herbivorous animals eat exclusively
vegetable matter; and omnivorous animals consume both
animal and vegetable matter.
Frog and toad larvae or tadpoles are either carnivorous,
omnivorous or herbivorous de-

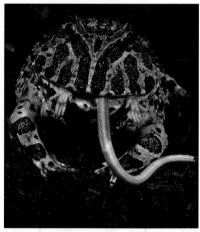

pending on the species. All fully transformed or adult stage frogs
and toads are carnivorous with the majority more accurately described as insectivorous or insect eater (although a vegetarian species has been recently reported). Larger species will consume other
types of animal matter, including arthropods other than insects
(for example, crayfish), fish and small mammals such as mice, small

41

birds, small snakes and lizards. Some species will even eat other frogs and toads, including members of their own species—which essentially makes them cannibalistic as well. The vast majority of all frogs and toads are stimulated to feed by sighting movement in their food. They do not consume dead or inanimate insects or animal matter, although a few species of toads have been observed eating dog food left outside for Rover. One technique you can try to feed dead prey to frogs is to wiggle it around in front of them, perhaps with a stick or other object, to induce a feeding stimulus.

Insects

It is best to feed *living* insects, such as crickets, fruit flies, spiders, earthworms, moths or other living creatures to frogs. Keeping frogs of different sizes together in the same enclosure fosters the likelihood of the larger frogs eating the smaller ones, so this housing arrangement needs to be carefully considered. Given the right temperature and humidity conditions, a healthy frog or toad is a voracious feeder that needs to be fed at least daily. A few smaller species require copious quantities of tiny insects on a daily or every other day basis. If three days go by without feeding them, such animals often die of starvation. This obviously causes a logistics problem for people thinking about owning such frogs, and they must ensure a steady food supply even during the winter months when feeder insect shipments are apt to arrive dead or dying from exposure to the cold. It is also an important financial consideration. After a few weeks of feeding a $5 frog, the costs of that feeding will begin to mount, and over the months and years, the cost of the food is apt to far exceed the original cost of the animal. The same can be said, of course, about any pet. The maintenance costs often surpass the acquisition cost, but many people neglect to consider this at the outset.

Possible solutions to this problem are to co-op large feeder insect shipments with other frog fanciers in your area, raising your own feeder insects and, when season permits, collecting your own bugs from areas that have not been treated with pesticides, herbicides, fertilizers or other potentially harmful chemicals. Regardless of how you choose to feed your frog or toad, be sure you budget appropriately for the feeding and upkeep costs or you will soon lose them. Many pet shops that sell frogs and toads also carry feeder insects, and this is an ideal source of picking up food for these animals in small, conveniently priced purchases when you need them. You may be able to obtain enough food on each visit to feed your animals for the whole week in the process.

Many pet shops sell feeder insects. This Barking Tree Frog happily eats grasshoppers.

The first questions you should ask your pet shop owner or dealer before you buy a frog or toad are what they have been feeding it and if they can assure you that they will always be stocking this food. Most pet shops are fairly reliable in what they warrant to their customers, but if you are not confident or are not familiar with their reputation, you should ask to see the animal eat before you plunk down your money and carry it home.

If your pet shop cannot supply you year-round with the appropriate live foods for your frogs, you will have to consider bringing them in by mail order. A list of live insect and small mammal providers is included in chapter 9.

Most of the time, raising and feeding tadpoles is an infinitely simpler affair. Vegetarian species can be fed small pieces of boiled lettuce, aquarium plants, like *Elodea* and others commonly available in pet shops, and occasional pieces of boiled spinach. Lighting their tank will also cause the growth of algae, which they also relish, and quite a few species will readily eat vegetarian and regular tropical fish food flakes of appropriate size. Carnivorous tadpoles can also be fed a variety of live fish foods, such as Daphnia, strained brine shrimp and aquatic worms. The tadpoles of some of the dart-poison frogs (*Dendrobates*) are more problematic and need to be isolated in small containers and carefully fed a drop or two of egg yolk from an eye dropper on a daily basis. Although labor intensive, acquiring the food material is obviously not difficult. Many species of tadpoles will attack and feed on weaker or dead brothers and sisters as well. It is important to feed tadpoles a variety of foods well endowed with vitamins and minerals necessary for proper growth. Failure to do so will result in retarded growth, improper development and an invariably fatal condition seen in the newly metamorphosed froglets known as spindly-leg syndrome. Some tadpoles are born with large yolk reserves and will not begin taking outside foods for several days. It is a good idea not to feed new tadpoles for a day or two and to watch them carefully to see if they are eating the food when offered. If not, the uneaten food will foul their container so it should be strained out or otherwise removed.

Live frog food dealers are listed in chapter 9. In addition, most pet shops that keep and sell frogs also stock a limited number of satisfactory food items.

FOOD OPTIONS FOR CAPTIVE FROGS

All species of frog or toad will eat bugs of any kind: crickets, sprintails, moths, worms, mealworms, super mealworms, ants, flies, termites . . . to name just a few. Larger frogs can be fed newborn and fuzzy mice, and a few really big species will gobble up fully grown mice. Frogs and toads are fairly indiscriminate eaters—if they really don't like a food item, they'll try it anyway and then spit it out. If this is the response, take that item off your list.

chapter 6

Housing
Your
Frog or Toad

Appropriate housing for your frogs and toads is one of your most important considerations when you are thinking about getting a pet. Much thought and planning should go into housing certain species. Some totally aquatic species do well in an ordinary aquarium setup and others can be kept in a tank of shallow water with a few smooth rocks for them to climb out on. Give serious thought as to how you will keep the water clean. Aquariums containing the

larger species or crowded with a number of frogs become fouled with the excreta rapidly. It may be necessary to set aside time each day to move the frogs to a temporary holding tank, change and clean

the primary tank and put them back in their regular
home. Also make sure that you have the minimal facilities to perform these tasks. Dirty tank water should be
flushed down the toilet or, alternatively, used to fertilize a flower bed (if available), and clean, aged water
should always be available to replace it.

The more elaborate and decorative your setup, the
more work it will be to tear down and clean. If you
choose to keep a very decorative setup, you should
consider keeping only a very few small species so as to
minimize labor time involved. You may be able to keep
a few small species in a large vivarium for weeks, a
month or even longer with a minimum of maintenance. Larger toads and water frogs, however, are best
housed in more spartan surroundings for the sake of
cleanliness and convenience.

The most convenient cage to use for any amphibian is
a store-bought all glass aquarium tank. Pick a size that
will not cause your frogs to become overcrowded and
make sure you get a screen cover rather than a glass
top. Enclosing such tanks in glass can cause the air to
stagnate, heat and humidity to build up and microorganisms to flourish. It is better to keep the cage airy
and provide humidity from an external source on a
regular or as-needed basis.

Ground Cover

If you want to use a substrate or ground cover, do not
buy any gravel or pebbles with sharp or angular edges.
Thin-skinned frogs will easily scrape themselves on this
material; such wounds can become infected and ultimately your animals could die. Decorative substrate
should be smooth, water-worn pebbles. The same prin-
ciple applies to rock formations: Avoid any sharp,
jagged or angular edges. All ridges and edges should
be smooth to prevent cuts and abrasions.

Many experienced frog and toad keepers find that
a layer of damp plain white paper towel is the best
material to use as substrate. It is easy to see soiling, can
be picked up, discarded and replaced easily and makes

the chore of cleaning and maintaining hygienic conditions far simpler than if you use gravel, pebbles, sphagnum moss or soil. Atop the substrate place an inner plastic bowl, such as a refrigerator food storage dish, with water in it for the frogs to soak or swim. If small frogs are being housed, make sure the water is shallow enough for the frog to sit in it without the head being underwater and that they can easily climb out. It may be necessary to give them "steps" in the form of small stones or rocks for this purpose. Frogs can drown also!

Burrowing species such as Spadefoot Toads and Narrowmouthed Toads need to be provided with a sterile soil substrate of sufficient depth to meet their natural requirements. Avoid silica sand and sharp, jagged-edge gravel, as substrates can irritate or even cut or abrade these thin-skinned species as they do what comes naturally for them—which is to dig down and bury themselves.

Terrariums for Land Dwellers

If keeping tree frogs and you wish to plant the tank for them, you need a tank that is high as well as wide and long. Use only sterile potting soil and sphagnum moss to lay down a layer of substrate for such vivaria. Tree frogs and mainly terrestrial species, such as toads, require a terrarium consisting of a dry or land portion and perhaps just a small pond, fashioned out of a plastic refrigerator dish of suitable size. A single small specimen could be kept in a plastic box with fitted screen cover, which is available in many pet shops. The only drawback to plastic is its propensity to become scratched, clouded and discolored over time. Glass can be cleaned more easily with no risk to surface damage unless you outright break it. Professional breeders and keepers, with no desire to attractively display their animals, resort to utilitarian plastic bowls and dishes commonly available in supermarkets and any large discount department store. These dishes come in every size, shape and height imaginable and often come complete with a fitted lid that can be

drilled to provide airholes and circulation. If you are
going to display your frogs, all-glass aquarium tanks
with fitted screen lids are your best option. You are
limited in size and shape options to mainly rectangular
or hexogonal structures of a variety of predetermined
widths, lengths and heights depending on the gallon-
age obtained. However, it may be possible for your
pet shop to order a special-sized tank that is custom
built to your specific dimensions. For example, you
may want to house a number of frogs over a wide
surface area but do not need the height afforded
by larger-sized aquariums that are available off the
shelf. On the other hand, you may want significant
height for tree dwelling species but may not require
the larger surface area ready-made fish tanks of such
heights contain.

If you wish to establish a decorative terrarium for your
frogs, you should use a layer of coarse pebbles first,
covered by sterile potting soil. Plant the soil with
desired plants, making sure those selected are not poisonous to your thin-skinned frogs or the insects they
eat, and cover the surface with a layer of orchid tree
bark to hold down the soil. The problem encountered
with a highly decorated and planted terrarium comes
from boisterous species that will fling dirt up onto the
glass side of the enclosure, uproot plants or crush
them and in general make maintenance a difficult
chore. If you are considering such a jungle setup, consider obtaining smaller, more delicate species of frogs
that would be less likely to make a mess of such a setup
on a daily basis.

Tree frogs have special housing needs. They can be
kept in simple enclosures with paper towel substrate
but also equipped with branches or pieces of high
driftwood on which to climb. They can also be accom-
modated in more elaborate planted terrariums, but
bear in mind that their weight may damage all but the
strongest or heavier stemmed varieties of live plants.
They could also be provided with artificial plants or
branches that can be removed, rinsed and wiped down
with plain water as necessary.

Aquariums for Aquatic Frogs

Strictly aquatic species can be kept in aquarium tanks. The African Clawed Frogs and the so-called Surinam Toad are examples of strictly aquatic species that never come up on land. They are strong swimmers and floaters and float at the surface to breathe but then dive and swim around more or less as if they were fish. Such setups should mirror any tropical fish setup. It can have an undergravel and external power filter, a screen cover with a light mounted above it, aquatic plants and other decorative items. It will need the same kind of maintenance as an aquarium tank, and how often you clean it depends on how rapidly it gets dirty. Obviously, the greater the number of frogs you keep in a single aquarium, the faster it will become fouled. It is important to make sure that the aquarium is large enough to house the number of frogs and to accommodate their size. The more frogs, the greater the necessary aquarium size. A rule of thumb is about $\frac{1}{2}$ inch of frog per gallon with a 10-gallon tank size minimum. Thus a 10-gallon tank could hold five 1-inch frogs or one 5-inch frog comfortably.

Different frogs require different types of housing— aquariums for aquatic frogs, terrariums for land dwellers and a combination tank for semi-aquatic frogs.

Aqua-Terrariums for Semiaquatic Frogs

The aqua-terrarium is for semiaquatic frogs, and there are a number of strategies for meeting the needs of these species. Semiaquatic frogs include most of the Ranid species and such popular hobbyist frogs as the Oriental Fire Bellied Toad (yes, another frog called a "toad"). The same rule, ½ inch of frog per gallon, also applies to semiaquatic species.

Using a regular aquarium tank, you can slope several pounds of gravel against one side and add water to the other, creating in effect a pool and a beach. Another more elaborate scheme is to have a piece of glass or Plexiglas cut to size and divide the tank into a land side and a water side with it. The land side could be created by filling that half of the tank with smooth pea gravel or water-worn pebbles. Soil is not recommended, as it would soon turn to mud and smear the glass sides. In both situations you would need to siphon out the water at least once every two days and replace it with clean water (see "Like Water for Frogs," below). Another way of providing for semiaquatic species is to fill a large (20-gallon plus) aquarium with water to a depth of 4 or 5 inches and then place good-sized rocks with ridges in the middle or at the ends so the frogs can haul out on to them. The rocks must rest on the bottom and extend at least ½ to 1 inch above the water level. A layer of pebbles should be provided in the tank to prevent the rocks from cracking the bottom of the aquarium. This setup has the effect of creating an island for your frogs with water all around it or to one side, depending on where you place the rock.

A few companies make ready-made pools, stoneware and even small, air-pump powered waterfalls that you can insert into your frog setup, greatly enhancing its appearance and making it more homey for its occupants.

A WORD ABOUT QUARANTINE

Many experts believe that all new frogs and toads brought into an existing collection should be quarantined in a separate holding tank, preferably located in a separate room or as far from existing specimens as possible. The function of quarantine is to prevent the transmission of any diseases from the newly arrived specimens to healthy frogs and toads in your collection. Whether quarantine for new arrivals is absolutely necessary for frogs and toads is a matter of debate among veterinary specialists. However, the practice cannot hurt, and all new frogs might best be observed in isolation for a week or so before coming into proximity with previous arrivals.

Any of the setups mentioned can also use external background scenes or insertable cork or molded plastic or foam backgrounds to help decorate the enclosure. These are available in most pet shops and are made to fit the standard-size aquarium tanks. These trappings are a matter of individual taste.

Like Water for Frogs

Water quality is important for frogs. Although some species may live in brackish, acidic or highly alkaline waters, captive frogs with few exceptions can be safely maintained in water with a neutral pH (7.0). Fecal wastes and urine rapidly acidify frog water so it must be either filtered vigorously or changed frequently. If tap water is used, it should be aged for a day or two so that chlorine dissipates. If bottled water is used, it is preferable not to use pure distilled water because distilled water is lacking in many beneficial trace elements and minerals that can benefit frogs. Therefore, if you buy your frog water, it is worthwhile opting for mineral spring waters. Naturally, do not use any "designer" waters lightly flavored with various fruits! And frogs are not likely to appreciate the tiny bubbles of seltzer either, although carbonated water can be used in an emergency for water bowl refills. Strictly aquatic frogs may be overwhelmed by the bubbles of carbon dioxide in bubbly water, so it should be avoided for use in the tanks of aquatic species.

Rain

Frogs and toads love rain, and rain is an important factor in stimulating them to mate and breed. Whether you intend to breed your frogs or simply intend to duplicate natural rain or mist several times a day, you may want to invest in a timer controlled rainmaking system, such as the Rainmaker Jr.™ system. This system comes with a reservoir, a water pump and a network of small plastic piping and nozzles through which water is forced under pressure. Aimed into your tank (through a tiny hole cut into the screen cover), you can literally make it rain on your frogs and toads, even if for a short period. Torrential downpours should be avoided, as the water really has no place to go once your substrate becomes saturated.

SPECIAL WATER CONDITIONS

Some species like special water conditions. If you do not know the needs of your particular frogs, a pH of 7.0 is safest. You can purchase natural chemicals (principally designed for aquarium fish) to lower the pH of your water. Research your frog's special needs if possible. The more frogs you keep in a given volume of water, the faster it will get dirty. Enlarging the size of your enclosure or cleaning it more frequently are the primary options; or trade off or sell your excess frogs if you could bear to part with them.

Heavy metals are often overlooked water contaminants that can impair, or even kill your frogs. Poisoning from these metals is often slow and insidious and little can be done to reverse it. Many plumbing systems may place trace amounts of copper, lead or zinc into the water. You can combat this by allowing the tap to run for several minutes before adding this water to your tank, which will allow for dissolved metals in the first spurts of water to be flushed away.

A BENEFIT OF TAP WATER

On occasion, frogs with skin infections or fungal growths have been successfully treated by maintaining them in chlorinated tap water for a period of a day or two. This practice is worth trying if you encounter these kinds of problems that might otherwise be ultimately fatal. Treating medical problems of frogs is covered in more detail in chapter 7.

REMEMBER THE FOLLOWING BASICS

Some general principles concerning water for frogs:

1. Water should always be kept clean. Filtration systems help to maintain clean water, but partial or complete water changes every other day (or a minimum of three times weekly) are critical.

2. Although frogs and toads need water, small frogs and baby frogs can and do drown. If keeping small frogs, make sure whatever setup you devise allows

them to easily haul out of the water and to sit with their rumps on the bottom keeping their heads above water. Call it a kiddy pool.

Temperature Control

Frogs and toads prefer moderate, cooler temperatures ranging from the mid-60s to mid-70s on the Fahrenheit (F) scale. Excessive heat, especially coupled with dryness, causes them to rapidly dehydrate and die. For this reason, many species of frog and toad are active only at dawn, dusk or at night. During the hottest parts of the day, most species are hiding somewhere staying cool. Even tropical species from torrid countries in South America, Africa and Asia arrange their daily schedules to be active when temperatures drop into the low 80s or 70s F. Be mindful that a species from a country where the noonday temperatures reach a 100°F does not mean that your frog likes it that way. Nighttime temperatures may drop 20°F or more, and this is when your frog is likely to be most active.

A lighting fixture above your frog's tank can help provide heat.

It is necessary to accommodate the temperature needs of your frogs and toads. Glass aquariums used to house frogs and toads should never be sealed on top with a piece of glass or Plexiglas as this will cause heat to be retained and to build up. A tight-fitting and locking-type screen cover to keep your frogs from jumping or climbing out is best.

In the hot summer months, you may actually have to find a cool place to keep your frog tank, even if it

53

means using an air conditioner or household climate control system. In the cold months, if you allow your household temperatures to drop below 65°F, most frogs will become inactive. You may have to employ an undertank heating pad under a part of their enclosure during this period.

Other means of providing heat to frogs include the use of a low wattage incandescent lighting fixture and bulb. These bulbs are also available in red and blue colors for nighttime heating use. Hot rocks should never be used in a frog tank. The danger of electrical shock in a damp environment is simply too great. Moreover, use of these devices poses a serious threat of thermal burns to the delicate skin of frogs and toads.

Finally, you should also invest in a good quality thermometer that you can place in the tank tempor-arily to take a reading. If it is too hot (over 82°F) or too cold (under 65°F), modify the situation ac-cordingly. In emergency overheating situations, it can help to set up an electric fan and aim it at your frog tank for the duration of the heat spell. The circulation will help dissipate heat from the tank. The species accounts that follow will offer some temperature range guidelines where this information is known.

chapter 7

Frogs, Toads and Health

Unfortunately, veterinarians and other experts on frogs and toads (herpetologists) do not know enough about the diagnosis, care and treatment of their medical problems to establish a complete frog hospital just yet. However, considerable progress is being made in this area, thanks to the interest in these species from hobbyists, scientists and environmentalists seeking a medical reason for the mysterious decline of frogs and toads in the wild.

Frogs do get into medical problems, some of them quite serious and even fatal. The most common types of medical disorders are infectious diseases—bacterial, viral and fungal diseases. They also suffer from nutritional deficiencies, traumatic injuries and a vague set of disorders best described as "constitutional" diseases. The latter problems develop from improper housing, temperature or diet, resulting in stress, compromised immunity and failure to thrive. There is even a type of kidney cancer that is common in frogs, Lucke's Renal Adenocarcinoma, which is believed to be the result of such constitutional deficiencies. Many species of frogs excrete toxins that do not pose a problem for them or their brethren in the wild, but that can build up rapidly in the closed environment of a captive habitat. Notably, frogs and toads are unusually susceptible to pesticide sprays and cleaning agents used in their immediate vicinity, so great care should be taken to shield them from becoming poisoned by such agents. Cleaning of their water bowls, gravel or aquarium tanks should involve the use of plain hot water only. They should be wiped with fresh paper toweling as traces of detergent left on permanent towels could be left behind to trouble your frogs afterwards.

> **FROG AND TOAD FIRST AID KIT**
>
> 1. Betadine™ ointment
>
> 2. Neosporin™/Bacitracin™ ointment
>
> 3. Hydrogen peroxide
>
> 4. Small pair of mosquito forceps
>
> 5. Small pair of blunt-tipped tweezers
>
> 6. Sterile, disposable (non-powdered) gloves
>
> 7. 2 × 2 and 4 × 4 sterile gauze pads
>
> 8. Cotton-tipped applicators

If it becomes necessary to use a disinfectant on your frog-related surfaces, a diluted solution of hydrogen peroxide is among the most innocuous and can be thoroughly rinsed away with hot water afterwards.

Infectious Microbial Diseases

Infectious or contagious diseases, also referred to as microbial diseases, can be caused by viruses, bacteria, fungi and unicellular and multicellular parasites. Frogs and toads are susceptible to various types of all five categories of infectious diseases; however, some of these diseases are more prevalent in frogs and toads. Perhaps the most common bacterial disease of frogs is Red-Leg disease. Red-Leg disease causes the rear legs to become inflamed or reddened, and these germs ultimately attack the host organism's blood and internal organs. It is extremely difficult to treat and death is often inevitable. Red-Leg disease can, however, be prevented by keeping your frogs under extremely clean conditions, which, of necessity, means daily or every other day water changes. At least two types of bacteria have been implicated as the cause of this condition: *Aeromonas hydrophila* and *Pseudomonas aeruginosa*. These germs are common in the environment, but in the wrong place under stressful and unhygienic conditions, they can become deadly. In humans, under similar circumstances, they can also result in pneumonia and other serious infections. Although these germs are susceptible to a number of common antibiotics, there is virtually no information as to the proper doses to use in frogs and toads and what the best route of administration would be. If the signs of Red-Leg are caught early enough, it may be worth trying tetracycline ointment externally over the infected areas. This is a prescription item that your veterinarian would have to provide. You can also try over-the-counter antibiotic ointments such as Bacitracin™ and Neosporin™ or a combination ointment containing both ingredients.

An antibiotic ointment can help to alleviate external bacterial infections.

Another common germ of frogs and toads is *Salmonella sp.* Because frogs and toads eat bugs and bugs absorb *Salmonella* from the soil, it is not at all unusual to find this germ in the gastrointestinal tract of many frogs and toads. Kept in check by their immune systems, it is normal for them to carry this bacteria and it should not be treated—treatment could pose an unacceptable risk to the animal because so little is known about antibiotic dosages for frogs. Frogs who become stressed, usually as a result of unfavorable captive conditions, become immunocompromised. Should this occur, the *Salmonella* bacteria could overproduce, resulting in severe diarrhea and dehydration leading to death.

Fungal diseases are rarer than would be expected in an animal that lives in moist, dark and dampened environments. Most fungi attack open wounds, cuts or abrasions in frogs, so any sign of these should be rapidly attended to in order to prevent fungal invasion.

As fungal diseases are external, it may be possible to treat them externally with antifungal ointments and these should be tried. Such diseases are also susceptible to externally applied tropical fish nostrums, such as the dye malachite green. Fungi appear as feathery or fluffy whitish/grayish masses of material. Once fungi attack internal structures or start traveling via the bloodstream, they become extremely difficult or impossible to treat.

Little is known of viruses that affect frogs but there are a few pathogenic types specific to this group of animals. Scientists have even considered using the spread of these diseases as "weapons" in the fight against introduced species of frogs that are overrunning foreign habitats, such as the Marine/Cane Toad in Australia.

Wild-caught frogs and toads have a variety of internal unicellular and multicellular parasites (endoparasites), such as tapeworms, nematodes or roundworms and flukes, as well as a variety of amoebas and similar protozoans. Although there are known agents that will kill various endoparasites, little is known of their effect on frogs, the seriousness of their side effects on frogs, if any, as well as proper dosages. Endoparasite infections should be treated by a veterinarian, preferably one who is experienced with amphibians or who will access the information through networking with other informed veterinarians.

Occasionally, frogs and toads (particularly wild-caught) are found with ectoparasites such as leeches, which can be picked off with a pair of tweezers. The resulting wound should be disinfected with Betadine™ ointment.

Nutritional Disorders
METABOLIC BONE DISEASE

Lack of proper diet, or lack of a diet closely resembling that of the wild frog or toad, is the cause of a number of serious afflictions. These include spindly-leg syndrome, as well as its relative, metabolic bone disease. Frogs fed a diet containing insufficient amounts of calcium and phosphorus, particularly during development and growth periods, often suffer from this disease. Among the more important nutrients needed to prevent this disorder is vitamin D_3. Several times a week, it is a good idea to dust crickets with a supplement containing this vitamin.

The earliest signs of metabolic bone disease in frogs and toads are difficulty in stalking, grabbing and swallowing their food. Any frog that was able to do this before and suddenly seems to be having trouble trying to eat is probably starting to develop weaknesses in its bones and muscles, which negatively impact on its ability to secure and eat food.

Whether or not frogs and toads need full spectrum lighting to help them synthesize vitamin D_3 in their skin as reptiles do is still largely a matter of debate. However, it may prove worthwhile, (mainly for daytime active, diurnal, species), to provide several hours of full spectrum lighting over your frogs' enclosure. Species that remain in hiding during the day or that are active principally at night (nocturnal) or during natural hours of low sunlight probably would not benefit from man-made full spectrum lighting. Some researchers feel that full spectrum lighting helps to stimulate breeding in some species and, of course, it promotes plant growth should you be using live plants in your terrarium or aqua-terrarium. On the other hand, excessive ultraviolet light has been blamed for killing some types of frog eggs and causing extinctions and near extinctions in the American northwest, so it is not recommended for developing eggs. The impact of man-made and excessive lighting is an area that has engendered much controversy, and it is not possible to make recommendations that would apply to all frogs.

INTESTINAL OBSTRUCTIONS

A trip to the veterinarian is probably in order if your frog suffers from an intestinal disorder.

Another dietary-related condition is intestinal obstruction or fecal impaction, which usually occurs when frogs swallow gravel or sand along with their prey items. Occasionally even a small, rounded piece of gravel can cause this condition, but one should definitely avoid placing food items on such substrates, which will adhere to the prey and cause intestinal problems in the frog. Another cause of intestinal obstruction in some species is a steady diet of hard-shelled insects, such as beetles or their chitinous larvae (mealworms). Mealworms are a permissible food but they should not be given to the exclusion of softer-bodied insects in the diet.

Veterinary treatment, including surgical removal of the blockage, may be required. Before resorting to surgery, your veterinarian may try force-feeding a small dose of lubricating material, such as mineral oil, to see if this helps move the blockage though the animal's digestive system.

Among the constitutional symptoms of dietary or habitat deficiencies are excessive periods of time where your frog appears lighter or darker in color than usual, weak hind legs, a weak jaw, failure to eat, absence of defecation, inactivity or lethargy in a normally active species (some species normally sit still for long periods of time, such as the Horned Frogs) and the appearance of unusual skin secretions (don't touch them as they could be toxic). Faded colors in some species are an indication of a dietary deficiency best remedied by supplementing feeder insects dusted with a vitamin/mineral supplement.

Traumatic Injuries

Cuts and abrasions in frogs and toads are best treated by application of Betadine™ ointment once or twice daily until healing or scarification is observed. External lesions can also be treated with sterile gauze soaked in full strength hydrogen peroxide, which will produce local disinfection. Broken bones and major injuries that result in internal bleeding and loss of a limb, foot or digit are often fatal. Frogs that do recover suffer from lifelong disabilities.

DON'T OVERFEED YOUR FROGS

Overfeeding large carnivorous species such as Horned Frogs, Marine Toads and the Bullfrogs, especially on small mammals, such as mice or rat pups, can cause obesity and in some cases a build-up of fatty plaque. In fact, this type of diet has been blamed for blindness in the White's Tree Frog, a popular large pet species. Keep an eye on your frogs and toads to make sure that they don't get too plump.

Chemical Intoxications

As alluded to previously, there are many substances in the human environment that are dangerously toxic to frogs. These include soaps, detergents, surface disinfectants, pesticides, herbicides, fertilizers, paints, heavy metals, petroleum products and so on. It is important to keep your frogs' enclosure as isolated as possible from these kinds of environmental contaminants. Remember that a small amount of these substances can have a serious impact on your frogs' health, although the same amount would not bother you or your larger pets. Such materials may be, at least in part, responsible for the disappearance of frogs in the wild, and they are certain to kill your animals.

Life Span in Captivity

The study of the natural life span of both captive and free living frogs and toads is an uncertain science about which very little is known. In the wild, it is difficult to mark young froglets and track them over time, although researchers are experimenting with a variety of electronic devices such as tiny subcutaneous "pit" tags that emit a radio signal on a particular frequency. Captive frogs and toads can live for many years and some species of Bufo and the Argentinian Horned Frogs (*Ceratophrys sp.*) have been known to live fifteen to twenty years in captivity. Even delicate, difficult to maintain tiny species such as the dart-poison frogs (*Dendrobates sp.*) have been known to reach the ripe old age of fifteen years under ideal captive conditions. However, some species may live only a few years, and there are no clear and convincing records regarding the normal and expected life span of most frogs and toads. A Marine Toad (*Bufo marinus*) is alleged to have lived thirty-five years in captivity and only died as a result of an unexpected accident, not "natural causes."

One way to ensure the long life of your frogs and toads is to be sure that they cannot escape from their housing. Captives that escape from their microenvironments are often doomed because of dehydration and lack of food and often are found dead and shriveled up days, weeks or months after they were known to be missing. Keeping your frog enclosure secure is essential in protecting your frogs against this type of mishap.

Handling Frogs and Toads

Frogs and toads should not be handled frequently or at all, although circumstances will arise where it may be necessary to handle them. These might include examining them, treating cuts and bruises, moving them from their regular home to a holding tank while cleaning their main home and taking them to the veterinarian or to the frog show.

The following is a short list of some of the handling tools you should have on hand should it be necessary to handle your frogs or toads:

1. At least two clean fine-mesh nylon fishnets. Size should be large enough to accommodate your largest frog.

2. A pair of clean, never used plastic or wooden chopsticks.

3. An 8-inch length of clear plastic tubing ¾ to 1 inch in diameter. This can be purchased in most pet shops as such tubes are used as returns for under-gravel filter systems. Also find two corks or caps that fit snugly on the end of this tubing. You will need this tubing if you keep and need to handle tiny frogs of less than 1 inch in length.

4. Clear, clean plastic refrigerator food storage dishes with predrilled airholes that can be used as temporary holding containers or transport boxes for your frogs.

5. A box of disposable surgical gloves. These must be unpowdered and, if you're sensitive to latex, then they must be latex-free. Use gloves whenever doing dirty cleaning chores associated with your frogs. After you're finished, dispose of the gloves properly and wash your hands with soap and hot water.

Wash your hands thoroughly with soap and water both before and after handling any frog.

Prior to handling any frog be sure to wash your hands and rinse them vigorously to remove all traces of soap. Don disposable powder-free gloves if at all possible. Frogs larger than 1 inch in length should be scooped up in one fishnet and quickly covered over with a second net to prevent them leaping out of the net. They

can then be coaxed into a smaller holding container
while you work on their regular quarters or transport
them.

Very tiny frogs, such as the dart-poison frogs and other
small species, should never be picked up. It is too easy
to harm such small delicate creatures by holding them
in the hands. This is where the 1-inch diameter clear
plastic tubing comes in. With one end corked, place
the open end near the frog and gently coax it to hop
into the tube with a chopstick. When it is well inside
the tube, quickly cap the entrance end as well. You can
now examine the froglet at close range, even applying
a magnifying glass to see tiny structures, without even
touching it. The tube trick can also be used to transport these tiny frogs from one container to the next. If
you intend to keep the frog in the tube for five minutes
or more make sure that you have punched a few small
air holes in the plastic beforehand.

If it is necessary to hold larger species, the best way is
to grasp them around the waist, restraining in effect
their rear legs in a straight and downward position.
Even then some frogs are quite slippery and will try
and get away from you—and some will succeed. It takes
a certain amount of practice to know exactly how
much force to exert. Too much force can obviously
harm the frog, too little force can permit it to escape.
Most frogs and toads do not like being held. The
thought, if any, that must be racing through their
minds is that they are going to be eaten at any
moment. This causes them to be less than ceremoni-
ous in your presence, and they will urinate or even
defecate on you in a bid for you to drop your attention
and give them a moment to abscond. Do not be star-
tled by this, and stand your ground regardless of the
insults your frog or toad may heap upon you. Some
frogs, on the other hand are quite placid and still-
standing and will gladly perch on your open hand
for prolonged periods without worrying about their
safety. Tree frogs, in particular, are fond of attaching
themselves to one's hand or arm as it gives them a
perch well above ground level and this is their favorite

vantage point. This behavior is reminiscent of parrots and other trained birds.

If it is necessary to transport your frog, place its carrying case in a thermo-insulated Styrofoam cooler to protect it against temperature shifts if there are temperature extremes outside.

Froggy Dangers to People

Frogs are about the most innocuous and innocent members of the animal kingdom and serve overwhelmingly to help, not hurt, human beings. Nonetheless, some frog species are dangerously poisonous—capable of secreting toxins that are characterized as among the most poisonous substances on earth. Every recorded incident of one of these toxins poisoning or killing a human has been related to foolish and risky behavior. In one recent spate of cases in New York City, a number of young men swallowed a Chinese drug known as Shen Su, which was supposed to be applied externally. It contained dangerous bufotoxins, or toad poisons, and several men died and others were hospitalized in critical condition. Fraternity pranksters on occasion make pledges swallow goldfish, but when toad licking was a substituted activity there were near deadly consequences. Serious hobbyists, aware of the dangerous secretions some species have, have never been harmed by their frogs thanks to careful precautions. Under no circumstances should a tadpole, frog or toad be placed in the mouth or swallowed. Frogs' legs are thoroughly cleaned, the skin removed and then they are cooked. Even then only certain species of frogs' legs are safe to eat, and on occasion improperly cooked legs have caused parasite infections in the people who ate them.

Although ninety-nine percent of the 4,500 plus frogs in the world do not bite humans, there are a few species with sharp, frontally situated teeth that could give an unwary handler a nasty cut (and that would be the worst of it). These species include the popular Horned Frogs (Pac-Man Frogs) and the African Bullfrog (*Pyxiecephalus sp.*). Make sure that all skin-breaking frog bites are thoroughly disinfected and seek medical attention quickly if they become swollen, inflamed, painful or tender. No frog can deliver a poison via its bite but there may be harmful bacteria present in the frog's mouth that could be introduced into the bloodstream via a bite wound. As a matter of first aid, all animal bites should be thoroughly washed in soap and hot water and then disinfected by soaking in a basin of Betadine™ solution for an hour or more. If this is not possible, quickly wash the bitten area and at least apply the disinfectant and dress the bite with a sterile bandage.

A horned frog's bite will probably not be serious, but should be quickly washed and disinfected.(albino Chaco Horned Frog)

Rarely will a pet frog develop a form of cutaneous tuberculosis known as *Mycobacterium marinum.* This disease causes large granulomatous lesions on the skin and it is contagious to humans. If a frog has any strange looking skin lesions or bumps, be sure not to touch them with bare hands and to seek veterinary attention quickly. If you have touched the lesion, check with your doctor, who can determine if you have become infected. The condition is readily treatable and is never fatal. Fisherman get it from handling infected fish and even swimmers get it from swimming in contaminated swimming pools. In fact, for this reason it is sometimes called Swimming Pool Granuloma. Infectious diseases such as this, transmittable from animals to humans, are called zoonotic diseases.

In addition to *Mycobacterium marinum,* frogs may also harbor *Salmonella, E. coli, Pseudomonas* and *Aeromonas,* as well as a variety of protozoan and fungal microorganisms that can also infect humans. However, because frogs and toads really serve as exhibit animals and should be handled cautiously and infrequently, such diseases are rarely a problem for humans. Those at most risk are children under eight years of age, pregnant women and people who are immunocompromised for any reason. Such people should avoid contact with animals such as frogs and toads. In households containing high risk people and frogs, caretakers of the frogs should be diligent in washing thoroughly after handling the frogs or doing frog-related chores such as cleaning out water bowls or dropping in food. Direct contact with the animal is not necessary for someone at risk to be infected. Germs are most commonly carried on the hands of the person in contact with the frog, who passes them to the next person by touch or to food and eating utensils.

The
Variety
of

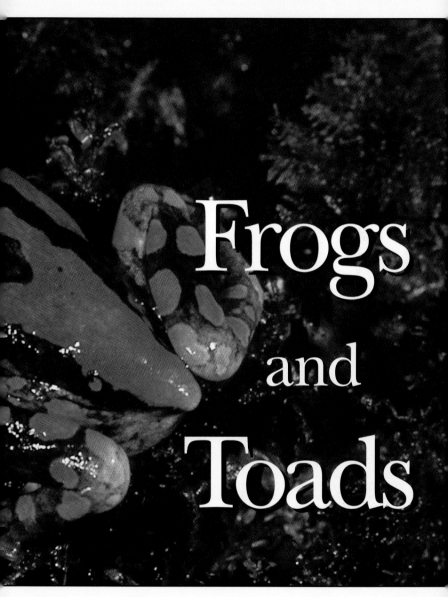

part three

Frogs and Toads

chapter 8

A Frog or Toad for You

Containing some forty-one families, hundreds of genera and thousands of species, only those groups that commonly find their way into the hobbyist trade, and of these only the most popular and/or most commonly available species, will be discussed here. Thus, this section is arranged by family, genus within each family often kept as captives, followed by a brief description highlighting the more important captive-care considerations of selected species within the family presented.

Family Discoglossidae

The Discoglossidae family of frogs (whose name means disk-tongue or flat-tongue) is also known as the painted frogs. These include:

1. *Alytes* found in western, central and southern Europe and northwestern Africa. There are three species, all of which are known as the midwife toads.

2. *Barbourula* with only two species found in northern Borneo, the Philippines and Palawan. These are known as jungle toads.

3. *Bombina.* Six species are known, ranging from western Europe to Turkey, Ukraine, eastern Asia, Russia, China, Korea and Vietnam. Commonly referred to as the fire bellied toads, some species are more colorful and popular than others. One species has a yellow underbelly and has interbred with fire bellied forms to produce an orange bellied hybrid in the Danube Valley, Austria.

   All members of this group are commonly seen in the hobby and a number of species are bred in captivity. The Oriental Fire Bellied Toad (*Bombina orientalis)* is the most common and popular member of the family.

4. *Discoglossus* or painted frogs. There are three species found in parts of southern Europe, northwestern Africa, Israel and Syria.

PAINTED FROGS

The Painted Frog (*Discoglossus pictus*) and some five other species of this genus are found in southern Europe (Portugal and Spain), Israel and on Corsica and Sardinia. The Israeli species, *Discoglossus nigriventer,* or Black Bellied Painted Frog, is near extinction and few members of this family, other than *D. pictus,* are readily available in the United States.

This species sports a variety of colors and patterns and, despite its name, might appear rather drab by comparison to other species. It requires an extremely large enclosure and eats a variety of small insects including crickets, chopped earthworms and aphids.

MIDWIFE TOADS

The Olive Midwife Toad (*Alytes obstetricans*) and the other two members of its genus, the Brown Midwife

Toad (*A. cisternasii*) and the Majorca Midwife Toad (*A. muletensis*), are best known for the active role of the father in caring for a mated pair's eggs. The Olive Midwife Toad is found in western Europe, the Brown variety in Portugal and, of course, the Majorca Midwife Toad from the Spanish offshore island of Majorca. This island form was discovered only in 1979 due, no doubt, to the fact it is found in fairly remote, mountainous habitats.

Olive Midwife Toad

The Olive Midwife Toad is well established in Great Britain and elsewhere in Europe. It is a small species requiring small- to medium-sized insect fare and a large terrarium with a removable pool or pond in the form of a sunken plastic dish (clean and refill daily). This toad prefers cool, damp conditions with temperatures ranging from 65° to 75°F. Free-ranging outdoor breeding colonies of these unique toads have been established in several locations in the United Kingdom (U.K.). Given the fascinating nature of their life history, numerous attempts have been made to breed this species in captivity but have failed to produce any results.

FIRE BELLIED TOADS

Fire bellied toads can endure a wide range of temperatures between 65° and 80°F. They are a relatively small species reaching 2½ to 3 inches in snout-vent (s-v) length and should be housed only with similar-sized members of their own species. Fire bellied toads are voracious eaters and will even attempt to eat smaller members of their own species. Similar-sized frogs will try to swallow the arms and legs of tankmates when food is crawling nearby!

Fire bellied toads should not be mixed with other species because they secrete a toxin known as bombesin that could harm or even kill other species. In fact, their secretions can build up in tank water and possibly harm themselves, which is why their semi-aquatic enclosure should be carbon filtered with fifty percent water changes at least every two days and complete water changes at least once a week. They will eat a wide variety of insect matter including earthworms, mealworms, crickets and fruit flies. Larger earthworms should be chopped into conveniently sized pieces—they will continue to wriggle and attract the attention of the frogs.

Yellowbelly Toad (right) and European Fire Bellied Toad (left).

These are attractive, easy to keep and lively little frogs that are best housed in at least a filtered 10-gallon (or larger) aquarium landscaped with rock formations. A screen cover is necessary to prevent these frogs from either climbing or jumping out of the tank. A low-wattage incandescent or full spectrum fluorescent lighting fixture can be turned on for several hours a day. They are readily available and many hobbyists and professionals are captive-breeding them both for the pet trade and for medical research, as their skin secretions have important medical applications and are even being investigated for the treatment of gastrointestinal problems and some kinds of cancer in humans. Members of the genus *Bombina* are active both day and night and can often be seen basking in the sunlight, an unusual behavior for frogs but quite common in reptiles.

Yellowbelly Toads
The Yellowbelly Toad (*Bombina variegata*) is a native of Europe. It has a greenish back and a yellow underbelly

interspersed with blotches of black. This species grows
to about 1½ inches.

They can be fed any insect small enough for them to
swallow. You may try to feed them some live tropical
fish foods such as tubifex or white worms if available; if
not, half-grown crickets, fruit flies and small mealworms are a good choice. Like all frogs, they should be
fed at least once daily.

These little frogs foul their tank water rapidly even
with an excellent filtration system, so several times
a week about half of the water should be siphoned off
and replaced. About every ten days it is necessary to do
a complete water change as well as to clean out the filter system.

European Fire Bellied Toads
The European Fire Bellied Toad (*Bombina bombina*) is
found in northern Europe. It is also a small species
and resembles the Yellowbelly save for the different
color of its belly. Care is basically the same.

*European Fire
Bellied Toad.*

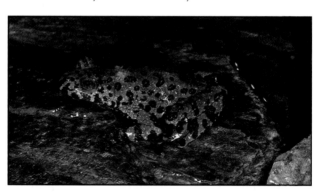

Oriental Fire Bellied Toads
The Oriental Fire Bellied Toad (*Bombina orientalis*) is
found throughout northeastern Asia. It is exported in
great numbers from China and appears regularly in
the pet trade; however, local captive-born specimens
are the best choice when obtaining these beautiful
little frogs. They are bright green and black above and
their bellies sport a bright red and black pattern. They
reach a length of about ·2 inches and should have

plenty of space—two adults should have at least a 10-gallon aquarium to play in, and larger groups need correspondingly larger aquariums.

*Oriental Fire
Bellied Toad.*

They can be fed a variety of insects that should be dusted with a good vitamin/mineral supplement containing carotene, which this frog needs to maintain its beautiful red coloration. Most captive-reared insects are apt to be raised on bland meals and culture media that do not contain this essential element. You could also try feeding food insects carrots or other yellow veggies to "gut-load" them with carotene before feeding them to the frogs.

Giant Yunnan Fire Bellied Toads

The Giant Yunnan Fire Bellied Toad (*Bombina maxima*), which is slightly larger than the Oriental Fire Bellied Toad, is occasionally available in the pet trade. It prefers deeper waters to swim around in (8 to 10 inches deep), so larger aquariums need be employed. These toads also require rafts or rock formations in their housing so that they can come out of the water to feed and bask in the light. This species prefers cooler temperatures (in nature, it ranges from southern China to eastern Siberia), and will remain active at temperatures as low as 50°F.

Giant Yunnan Fire Bellied Toads will eat larger insects such as half-grown to three-quarter-grown crickets,

75

mealworms and flies. Gut-loading such bugs with carotene or dusting them with a good vitamin supplement
helps these frogs to maintain their vivid red underbelly.

There are several other species of fire bellied toad
from inside China, but these are never exported to the
U.S. These include the Hubei and the Guangxi Fire
Bellied Toads.

Family Leiopelmatidae

This family of frogs contains just two living genera—
the Tailed Frog (*Ascaphus truei*) of the northwestern
U.S. and southwestern Canada and three species of the
genus *Leiopelma,* which are confined to New Zealand
and never enter the pet or hobbyist trade. Occasionally
the so-called Tailed Frog is available. This is the only
species of frog that engages in true sexual intercourse,
although the three species of New Zealand frogs also
engage in internal fertilization of ova but do so by cloacal contact, very much like the method that birds use
to fertilize eggs.

These are small frogs, reaching lengths of less than
1 inch. The Tailed Frog is primarily an aquatic species
and should be kept in an aqua-terrarium at relatively
cool temperatures in the 65° to 75°F range. They can
be fed small-sized crickets, tubifex worms and aquatic
insect larvae.

Family Bufonidae

The Bufonidae family is the family of the so-called true
toads. It is a huge family with more than twenty genera
and over 300 living species. The largest group are the
toads in the genus Bufo with more than 200 species.
Many of the true toads are excellent starter species.
They live mainly on land, going to water only to breed
and occasionally to take in water through absorption
from their dorsal surfaces. One bufonid, the Malayan
Climbing Toad, is found in low-lying brush and trees.
Bufonid toads are found throughout the world. Toads
can be easily housed in an aquarium tank with a plain
white paper towel substrate or, if you do not mind

cleaning it off the glass regularly, some sterile potting soil. They need a large, shallow dish of water, which should be cleaned and replaced at least once a day. If you luck onto a Malayan Climbing Toad, a few branches to climb would make it feel right at home.

What one feeds a Bufo toad depends mainly on the toad's size. Large Bufo toads, and there are a number of them, can eat small mice without a problem. Some large toads have been observed gobbling up dog food left outside houses in bowls for a yard dog. It is not, therefore, a good idea to leave dog food outside in areas populated by such species as the dog, as often as not, comes along and bites the toad, releasing its glandular poisons. (The principal glands containing toxic substances are located above the toad's shoulders to the rear of the eyes.) If swallowed, the poison could kill the dog. Moreover, dog food is not designed for toads and could cause dietary deficiencies or excesses that will ultimately affect the toad's health. Smaller species of toads will also eat all manner of insects including crickets, mealworms, super mealworms, moths, flies, beetles and spiders— virtually anything that they can swallow including other frogs, lizards and even small snakes.

Colorado River Toad.

Large toads in the 6- to 8-inch range include the Marine Toad, the Blomberg's Toad and the Colorado River Toad (*Bufo alvarius*). The Colorado River Toad is becoming very scarce throughout most of its range, and it is becoming increasingly difficult to find these animals, although specimens are still available on occasion. This is a large toad that is definitely worth breeding because of its increasing scarcity and its pretty markings (making it popular as a pet): slate gray, glossy rhinolike skin with orange spots.

77

Common American Toads and other small to medium-sized species in the 2- to 5-inch range can be fed crickets, mealworms on occasion (not as a steady diet), earthworms, moths, flies and beetles. Such toads are still very populous in many locations, and you can try your hand at collecting a few yourself (check local game laws first). These are a great starter species and cost either nothing or very little if you buy them.

Primarily terrestrial in nature, toads can be kept either in elaborate terrariums with water dishes large enough to accommodate them (clean daily or twice daily) or in simple aquariums with paper towel as substrate and a water dish. Although toads come from a large number of different climatic conditions, virtually all can be successfully kept in the 70° to 80°F range. They generally abhor great heat, and in the wild can often be found dug into the moist substrate in the shade during the hottest part of the day. They are most active at cooler times, such as at dawn, dusk and at night, and can often be found around suburban homes with insect-attracting lights. The toads lie in wait in the shadows to feast on the bugs drawn to such lights as they fall to the ground.

There are five domestic bufonid toads on the national U.S. endangered species list: the Houston Toad, the Puerto Rican Crested Toad, the Wyoming Toad, the Southwestern Arroyo Toad and the Sonoran Green Toad. The U.S. also protects an additional seventeen frog and toad species, many of them from overseas locations, and the CITES list is larger still. But with all the thousands of different frogs and toads, it still leaves a very large selection for hobbyists to keep and study. And if you are fortunate to get a rare or endangered species, usually from captive-bred stock, then this would be the one to try breeding yourself.

POPULAR AMERICAN BUFO TOADS
American Toads
The American Toad (*Bufo americanus*) is the most common toad of the eastern U.S., ranging from the tip of

New England south to northern Georgia, and across the midwest from Minnesota to Mississippi. It is also found throughout central and northeastern Canada.

This species prefers cool, moist habitats and is active principally at night and on cool, overcast days and at dusk and dawn. It eats virtually any kind of bug it can find and is a voracious feeder. In fact, it is reliably estimated that a single adult American Toad swallows up to 100 insects a day, 3,000 a month and nearly 10,000 over the course of a single summer season. It has few natural enemies, but one, the

Sonoran Green Toad.

Hognose Snake, speciaizes in eating such toads and does not seem deterred by the toad's poisonous gland secretions. Other toad predators have learned to flip them on their backs and eat them from the belly, studiously avoiding the poison glands on their dorsal surfaces.

American Toad.

A single adult or pair of these toads can be housed comfortably in a 10- to 15-gallon terrarium with a water dish and a plain paper toweling substrate or a bottom layer of pebbles and potting soil atop it. A water dish large enough to accommodate all the members of the toad tank should be provided and emptied and refilled at least once daily.

Southern Toads

The Southern Toad (*Bufo terrestris*) is found throughout the southeastern U.S. from coastal Virginia through Florida and westward to Louisiana. Southern

Toads appear at home in sandy areas, remain burrowed just beneath the surface and come out at night to forage or mate. Like the American Toad, it will eat virtually any animated insect prey.

If kept in a landscaped terrarium, a sandy loam or potting soil is best. A water dish to one side should be provided for the toad to soak; this must be changed daily.

Southern Toad.

Fowler's Toad.

Fowler's Toads

The Fowler's Toad (*Bufo woodhousi fowleri*) is a subspecies of the Woodhouse's Toad and is found throughout the eastern half of the U.S. westward to the Mississippi. The subspecies is named after an early Massachusetts field biologist named S. P. Fowler. The primary species, a more western ranging species, *Bufo woodhousi,* is named in honor of an early southwestern surgeon and explorer named Dr. Samuel Washington Woodhouse. Their care and housing requirements are virtually the same as those for the American Toad.

Red Spotted Toads

The Red Spotted Toad (*Bufo punctatus*) is found in the arid southwestern U.S. and shares its habitat with the Spadefoot Toads (see "Family Pelobatidae," later in this chapter). It is a small (about 3 inches maximum s-v length), pretty species dotted with red spots against a

Red Spotted Toad.

slate gray background. A terrarium carpeted with sandy soil and a melange of stones or rocks is ideal for this species. It prefers temperatures in the 70° to 80°F range. Like other bufonid toads, it will eat a wide variety of lively animated insect prey of suitable size.

POPULAR IMPORTED BUFO TOADS

Europe and Asia have their share of bufonid toads, some of which are occasionally imported into the U.S. The European Common Toad (*Bufo bufo*) is found throughout northern Europe and reaches about 6 inches in length; the Natterjack Toad (*Bufo calamita*) is a smaller species of about 4 inches in s-v length and the pretty Green Toad (*Bufo virdis*) reaches about 5 inches in length. Care for these three common European species is virtually the same. They require sandy soil or a plain paper towel substrate, a water dish and a terrarium of adequate size. They relish slugs, earthworms and most insects small enough to swallow whole. The Natterjack Toad is protected in most of its range throughout Europe as it is classified as a declining species in many areas where it was once plentiful.

The Java Toad (*Bufo asper*) and the Black-Spined Toad (*Bufo melanosticus*) are two common bufonids available from Asia. Both species prefer temperatures in the 70s. The Java Toad is the largest Asian Bufo, reaching lengths of approximately 8 inches.

*European
Common Toad.*

The Harlequin Frogs (*Atelopus sp.*) are another genus of bufonidae toads found in South and Central America.

They are beautiful, colorful toads with poisonous skin secretions. These species are becoming increasingly scarce and are subject to international protections. They do not thrive in captivity, although the few who have managed to obtain these toads have found that they were voracious eaters of small insects, like well-planted, well-ventilated cages and temperatures in the mid-70s.

*European Green
Toad.*

Family Dendrobatidae

The Dendrobatidae family includes the dart-poison frogs—so named because certain primitive Indian tribes in South America use the deadly skin secretions of these frogs to tip their hunting arrows or blow-gun darts. In spite of the fact that some of these species generate extremely toxic poisons and a few species generate sufficient amounts to kill hundreds of adult humans, not one hobbyist has ever been poisoned by one of these frogs.

Hobbyists have remained unharmed by these frogs for several reasons. Firstly, all dendrobatid frogs are now a regulated import and many are strictly protected by international treaties. All dendrobatid frogs appear on the U.S. endangered species list and most are listed on CITES Appendix II, limiting their importation. As a result, most of the frogs in the pet hobby are captive-bred and captive-bred frogs do not seem to have as deadly a group of poisons as their wild counterparts. This is undoubtedly related to their diet in the wild. Captive frogs are not fed the same insects that they would eat in their native forests, and the insects they are fed do not eat the same poisonous plants as the insects eaten by wild frogs. This is an example of how a deadly toxin works its way up the food chain. Insects eat poisonous plants and have miniscule amounts of these plant poisons in their bodies. The frogs eat thousands of these insects, obtaining the raw materials to synthesize far greater and far stronger toxins than even the insects or their plant food have. They have been jokingly referred to as "movable chemical factories."

In contrast, captive-bred and long-term wild-caught captives are fed innocuous insects that do not eat toxic plants, thus the frog, if it ever had a deadly skin toxin, soon loses the ability to make more of it. Obviously this is good news for hobbyists who worry about such things. Notably, however, not all frogs and not all toxins present in frogs are related to conditions in the wild. There are still plenty of captive-bred frogs and toads that are just as toxic as their cousins in the wild, so do not become complacent in handling these animals or allowing children or pets access to them. You can never really know unless you have a state-of-the-art biochemistry lab at your disposal.

The bright colors of the dendrobatid frogs are warning signals (known as aposematic coloration) to would-be predators that they harbor poisonous toxins and to stay away. Some of the less brilliantly colored dendrobatids do not seem to be as poisonous as their brightly-colored relatives and a group of them, the dull-colored Rocket Frogs (*Colostethus sp.*) are probably only mildly poisonous.

So what of frogs that are still very poisonous or frogs that were held by hobbyists/breeders before captive breds became widely available? The answer lies in careful handling. Handling such frogs with bare hands can be detrimental to the frogs as well as to the handler. See the discussion of handling in chapter 7 for tips on how to work with these little poisonous frogs so both you and the frog are suitably protected. There is a growing number of poison frog enthusiasts throughout the world, including many Americans. No dart-poison frog enthusiast should forgo membership in either the American Dendrobatid Group and/or the British Dendrobatid Group, two organizations that publish English-language newsletters with essential information for aficionados of these frogs (see chapter 9 for addresses). It is strongly advised that before one invests the money (dart-poison frogs are expensive—$25 to as much as $100 each), time and energy in these animals, they should become members of these two reasonably priced organizations for at least a year. Additional homework: Read all back issues of all available newsletters. The more informed you are, the better off you will be.

Armed with a thorough knowledge of these frogs, you might then consider buying a single or pair of a captive-bred (but less expensive) species to get your feet wet.

The amazing popularity of these frogs is due to their mystique, but also to their unbelievably beautiful colors and patterns. The fact that many of their toxic secretions are also being explored for their medical uses makes them no less interesting; and finally the amazing degree of parental care that they give their offspring makes it hard to believe these animals are mere frogs rather than birds or higher mammals.

There are approximately 160 species of dendrobatid in seven genera:

1. *Aromobates,* the Skunk Frog (aptly named and not a good choice for a household pet—it literally "stinks")—consists of one species.

2. *Colostethus,* the Rocket Frogs. This group contains more than 100 species, and although they have mildly poisonous skin secretions, they are dully colored and less popular than their more poisonous counterparts.

3. *Dendrobates,* the Dart-Poison Frogs, containing about thirty species—colorful but poisonous as wild living specimens.

4. *Epipedobates,* the Phantasmal Poison Frogs. This genus of frog is very colorful. A poison from their skin, epipedobatidine, is allegedly hundreds of times more powerful than morphine as a pain-killer, but it is nonaddictive and needs to be used in only extremely small doses to achieve results.

5. *Mannophryne,* the Fingered Poison Frogs, includes eight species.

6. *Minyobates,* the Tiny Poison Frogs, includes nine species.

7. *Phyllobates,* the Golden Poison Frogs with five species including one of the most poisonous, *Phyllobates terribilis,* a species that is not recommended to hobbyists. The poison of this species is extremely toxic and it purportedly can be absorbed through the pores of human skin. The other members of the genus *Phyllobates* are nearly as toxic. None should ever be handled bare-handed (see discussion of handling in chapter 7) and are best avoided by all except professionals involved in their scientific study. Whether it is correct to say that either long-term captives or captive-bred specimens of this genus are less poisonous or nonpoisonous is subject to debate. Clearly it is a chance that you do not want to take.

Dendrobatids are found in Central America. One species, the Green and Black Dart-Poison Frog

(*Dendrobates auratus*) was introduced into the upper Manoa Valley of Oahu, Hawaii, in 1932 for the purpose of mosquito control. The descendants of the original 206 specimens, collected from small islands off the Pacific Coast of Panama, still survive today in isolated populations in the moist valleys of Oahu. Studies of their poisonous skin toxins reveal that they differ markedly from the toxins secreted by their founders back in Panama, lending further credence to the theory that their poisons are somehow linked to their native diet or habitat.

Dart-poison frogs changing color. (Morphing Dart-Poison Frogs)

Dendrobatids are excellent climbers so they need to be secured in well-covered (screened over) terrariums. They are best housed singly or in pairs as their skin secretions can poison themselves and other species in the same container. They do best if provided with live plants, bromeliads or epiphytes (air plants). Although they are primarily arboreal, they also need moisture. A shallow water dish that they can easily climb in and out of (use small smooth stones as stepping blocks if necessary) should be provided. Change the water at least once a day to prevent build up of both waste matter and poisonous skin secretions. Be sure and flush the old water down the toilet; do not throw it anywhere where its poisonous nature may harm plants and animals. Take care not to spill or splash it around. It is recommended that you use disposable rubber gloves for this chore.

Replace the water with fresh, aged (dechlorinated) water after rinsing the dish, preferably with a good flushing of water from an outside hose with the effluent directed into a sewer drain.

Feeding dart-poison frogs is somewhat problematic. They are voracious eaters and given a steady supply of the right-sized bug they will eat incessantly during daylight. Providing a steady supply of small enough bugs is one of the most difficult chores a dart-poison frog keeper faces. It is estimated that a single adult dart-poison frog could easily consume about 100 ants or fruit flies a day, which means that anyone thinking about keeping these frogs should seriously think about establishing ant and wingless fruit fly cultures as well. They will also eat pinhead-sized crickets, which can be commercially purchased by mail order. A list of suppliers of live insect foods is included in chapter 9. Alternative food choices are termites, aphids, small fly larvae and other small bugs.

Experts advise that if you lose your source of food supply for two to three days, your frogs are certain to die—it is critical that you have food on hand. Going on vacation is also a problem unless you have someone reliable to take over your feeding and clean-out chores as well. Because of these demands, these are one group of animals most pet shops do not like to board. One alternative is to take your frogs and their food supply with you in small traveling plastic terrariums available in pet shops. Obviously there has to be a lot of strategic planning involved in such an effort. Some hosts may simply prefer that you leave your frogs and their bugs at home. Your only other option is to take a lot of day trips and when you get home at midnight rush in to feed your frogs and clean out their water bowl before you do anything

WHAT'S IN A NAME?

The poisonous denrobatid frogs are often mislabeled "Poison Arrow" or "Poison Dart" Frogs. The correct term for these frogs is "Dart-Poison" Frogs. The incorrect name implies that the frogs are darts themselves, when in fact they merely supply the poison for the dart. The early literature on these frogs was in foreign languages where the terms were correctly reversed due to the grammatical rules of those languages. Unfortunately the terms were then incorrectly translated and the error persisted.

else. Do the same thing early in the morning before
you depart.

Dendrobatids are particularly susceptible to a disease
called "spindly leg" syndrome, which is seen in newly
metamorphosed animals. It is believed that this mala-
dy is due to either nutritional deficiencies in the
mother frog or nutritional deficiencies in the food
that the tadpole is fed (or quite possibly both). Therefore, it is best to dust insects fed to these frogs with a
good vitamin/mineral supplement two or three times
a week. Such powdered preparations that stick to bugs
can be purchased in most full-line pet shops. Be sure
that the supplement you buy contains calcium, phosphorus and vitamin D_3 in addition to other trace elements and vitamins.

Because the dendrobatids are diurnal, tropical species,
it is safe to assume that they prefer light and warmth
(75° to 85°F) during the day, cooler temperatures at
night (70° to 75°F) and high humidity at all times. If
you set up a large terrarium for these frogs, use a
secure screen cover and manually mist it several times
a day. If you do not have time to mist, you may want to
purchase a device such as the Rainmaker Jr.™, which
has a programmable timer that turns on a pump and
forces water through tiny jets inserted through the
screening. In effect, the device automatically programs
periods of rain for your frogs. By well-planting your
terrarium, you also help to maintain humidity. Drop-
lets of water on leaves enable the frogs to absorb
needed moisture through their skin. Use artificial UV-
emitting light and avoid direct sunlight, which can
overheat the terrarium. If necessary, external sources
of heat can be provided by undertank heating pads
controlled either by thermostats or manually with the
judicious use of a thermometer.

Well-started, partly grown captive-bred frogs remain
relatively expensive compared to other species of frogs,
because raising the tadpoles and the tiny froglets is
quite challenging. Newcomers to dendrobatids should
not be too optimistic in this regard, but after years of

experience, patiently garnered, you may be able to make significant progress in this area.

POPULAR DART-POISON FROGS

Green and Black Dart-Poison Frogs

The Green and Black Dart-Poison Frog (*Dendrobates auratus*) is widely available from captive-bred stock and was the first and easiest of these frogs to breed in captivity. They grow to a maximum of 2½ inches in length. These frogs require a well-planted terrarium with a water bowl, hiding places and branches. The terrarium should have a secure cover. They eat a variety of small insects and are recommended for beginning dart-poison frog hobbyists. This species is native to Costa Rica and from Panama to western Colombia and has been introduced onto Oahu, Hawaii.

Blue Dart-Poison Frog.

Blue Dart-Poison Frogs

The Blue or Azure Dart-Poison Frog (*Dendrobates azureus*) is extremely beautiful and a great rarity because of its blue color—a color that is not common among frogs. It reaches about 1½ inches in length, eats small insects and is housed in the same fashion as all other dendrobatids. These frogs are being increasingly bred in captivity. The species was first discovered in 1969 in Surinam on the northern coast of South America.

Red and Black Dart-Poison Frog.

Yellow-Banded Dart-Poison Frog.

Red and Black Dart-Poison Frogs

The Red and Black or Harlequin Dart-Poison Frog (*Dendrobates histrionicus*) is a species best avoided by beginning dart-poison frog hobbyists as it is difficult to maintain in captivity. This species displays an amazing variety of patterns and color varieties. Some are black and yellow, some are black and red and yet others are orange and black. These frogs average about 1½ inches in length and are native to western Colombia and Ecuador.

Yellow-Banded Dart-Poison Frogs

This species (*Dendrobates leucomelas*) is a somewhat heavier and more robust member of the group, growing to about 1½ inches in length. It has bright yellow bands crowning the top of the head, extending vertically down the sides of the back on a jet black background. This frog will eat larger prey than most dart-poison frogs, and thus may be easier to feed. The Yellow-Banded Dart-Poison Frog ranges from Guyana to Venezuela. Its hearty constitution makes it a good frog for beginners.

Strawberry Dart-Poison Frogs

The Strawberry Dart-Poison Frog (*Dendrobates pumilio*) is a bright, metallic red-bodied frog that has black or mottled black and gray legs. This is a small species, reaching about 1 inch in length. It requires a steady diet of extremely small live insects such as aphids, ants and pinhead crickets. It is a difficult species to rear in captivity and is not recommended for beginners. It is native to Costa Rica and Panama.

Strawberry Dart-Poison Frog.

Dyeing Dart-Poison Frog.

Dyeing Dart-Poison Frogs

This species (*Dendrobates tinctorius*) is among the largest of this family of frogs reaching nearly 2½ inches in length. It has a number of highly variable color and pattern varieties mainly in the black, grayish-blue and

yellows. Because of its size when full grown it will eat
larger prey items such as half-grown crickets, small
moths and other small- to medium-sized insects. In the
wild, this frog lives throughout northern South
America in the Guyanas.

Family Centrolenidae

Known as the glass frogs, these species have translucent
skin. When viewed with a bright light in back of them,
you can see skeletal structures and other anatomical
structures very much as if you were looking at an
x-ray. There are three genera of glass frogs: *Centrolene*,
Cochranella and *Hyalinobatrachium* with approximately
eighty-five species. This is a group in which new species
are being discovered on a regular basis.

Glass Tree Frog.

They are rarely available in the pet trade as they fare
poorly in captivity and do not ship very well. If you are
lucky to get one of these oddities take good care of it.
Glass frogs need a well-planted terrarium with a substrate of damp sandy soil, a water dish and a steady supply of small insects. Most species are small, ranging in
size from ¾ to 3 inches, depending upon the species.
Many are colored green, lime green, yellow and yel-
lowish green. They are a slim, active species that need
to be fed daily and prefer temperatures in the high 60s
to low 70s, as they are found in cool, mountainous
regions.

If you encounter one of these frogs it is likely to be the Fleischmann's Glass Frog (*Centrolenella fleischmanni*), which has a wide range extending from southern Mexico, throughout Central America and over all of northern South America. A small, noncontiguous population also occurs in parts of northern Argentina and southern Brazil.

Family Hylidae

The family Hylidae or tree frogs is a large family of more than 750 species and even more subspecies, with new types being discovered and described virtually every month. It is among the most worldwide and cosmopolitan of the frog families with representatives found throughout North, Central and most of South America. Representatives of this clan also can be found in Australia, New Guinea, Tasmania and the Solomon Islands, as well as throughout most of Eurasia, China and Japan and coastal North Africa. They are present on many tropical islands, often stowing away in vessels to reach such locations.

Not all tree frogs live in trees. Some inhabit low-lying shrubs and some even spend time on the ground, although this is not true of most tree frogs. Many tree frogs do well around human dwellings and have no problem finding a home perched on walls, roof eaves, window ledges, doorway overhangs, drain pipes and other building structures. Tree frogs that live on the outside of houses soon learn about night lights and the bugs that they attract. So while toads remain on the ground to catch bugs that drop to earth, tree frogs creep along the walls, in the shadows near the lights waiting to feed upon the hordes of insects coming to the lights.

It is difficult to generalize about the housing requirements of tree frogs because they are such a diverse group. They require the usual appurtenances of an aquarium-type enclosure, screen cover, lighting fixture and substrate. Arboreal or tree living species should have sturdy branches on which to climb and perch in addition to potted or planted live plants. Pet shops now carry an assortment of driftwood and artificial branches that blend nicely in such setups or you can construct your own. Some species prefer vines to hang on, and where this is known it will be mentioned in the individual species accounts. A pool sunk into the substrate completes the picture; the water needs to be emptied, and the pool cleaned and refilled at least once a day.

Enclosures for tree frogs should have some extra height as well as surface area. Most tree frogs move about by walking, leaping and, in some instances, by what appears to be flying.

In general, tree frogs eat the same kinds of insects that all other frogs eat, but they are more apt to find their food perched along a branch or shrub rather than on the ground.

There are forty different genera of tree frogs, and not all of these are popular as pets or even available in the pet trade. The following groups are among the most interesting or most likely to be available.

Bird Voice Tree Frog.

1. *Acris,* a group consisting of the cricket frogs with two U.S. species and about five subspecies.

2. *Agalychnis,* the leaf frogs, the genus that is home to the ever-popular and hauntingly beautiful Red-Eyed Tree Frog discussed in some detail below.

3. *Gastrotheca*, the genus of the marsupial frogs. This group includes some forty species, several of which are usually available. These frogs are best known for their unusual life history and will also be discussed below.

4. *Hyla*, containing the true or common tree frogs. This is the largest genus of the Hylidae with some 300 or so living species.

5. *Litoria*, the genus of the Australasian Tree Frogs. Among this genus is the extremely popular, long-lived White's Tree Frog, discussed also in the species accounts.

6. *Osteopilus*, the Cuban Tree Frogs, of which at least one member has invaded the U.S.

7. *Pseudacris*, this genus is composed of the chorus frogs, with some thirteen species in North America.

CRICKET FROGS

There are two species and several subspecies of cricket frogs in the United States: the Northern Cricket Frog (*Acris crepitans*) and the Southern Cricket Frog (*Acris gryllus*).

Northern Cricket Frogs and Southern Cricket Frogs

Cricket frogs are named for their ability to jump around rapidly like crickets. Although a small species, their animated behavior dictates the need for a spacious enclosure. They eat a variety of small insects such as half-grown crickets, flies, mealworms and other bugs. These are a good, inexpensive species for the novice frog keeper if they are available. If you can maintain these frogs successfully, you can graduate to more exotic small frogs.

Northern Cricket Frog.

Cricket frogs prefer temperatures in the mid-60s to the mid-70s. They need a well-planted terrarium with plenty of hiding brush and a small pool of water, which should be changed daily. They are active primarily at night and this is when you may hear them calling.

LEAF FROGS

Red-Eyed Tree Frogs

The Red-Eyed Tree Frog (*Agalychnis callidyas*), is a spectacularly beautiful species that has become the poster-frog of the save-the-rain forest movement. Its photo can be found on calendars, posters and in innumerable magazine articles and coffee-table books on tropical rain forests. It is a member of a group of about ten species known as the tropical leaf frogs, which range from southern Mexico through Central America south to Ecuador along the Pacific coast of South America. The Red-Eyed Leaf or Tree Frog is found mainly on the Atlantic slopes and lowlands from central Mexico through northern Honduras and on the Caribbean slopes

Red-Eyed Tree Frog.

southward to Panama. This species lives in trees as high as 50 feet, but descends at nightfall during the rainy season to breed in ponds. They are often available in pet shops and from specialty breeders and importers.

The Red-Eyed Tree Frog grows to a maximum snout-vent length of about 3 inches and is lime green above with sides that are bluish-green with cream-colored bars and a cream-colored belly. Recently, a bright blue example of this frog was discovered, with orange feet and, of course, vivid bright red eyes.

One or a pair of these frogs need a spacious terrarium well-planted with broad-leaved plants, a substrate of sandy soil and a water dish. These frogs like high humidity, which can be achieved by placing a piece of glass over one-third of the screen cover. The remaining two-thirds should remain open so that poor ventilation and air stagnation is avoided. Misting several times a day will help maintain humidity and simulate their natural environment. This aspect of their care is essential, as they absorb almost all of their body water through their skin and will rapidly dehydrate or mummify, become inactive and die.

Because these frogs normally live at great heights they are more at home in a terrarium that is both spacious in area as well as higher than usual, such as a 55- or 60-gallon-high tank. They require temperatures in the mid-70s.

Experienced keepers say these frogs can become stressed rather easily, so they should not be handled unless absolutely necessary. In addition, it is advisable to feed only small numbers of insects at a time, making sure all the frogs get some. If you overfeed, the frogs will become overexcited and stressed as well. It can take weeks for these frogs to get settled into a new home, and they should be not be stimulated excessively or disturbed during this period.

This species is strictly nocturnal and spends the daylight hours "pasted" to the underside of a broad leaf frond or stuck in the corner of the terrarium. Set up a red night-light bulb so you can observe their activity at night.

Marsupial Frogs

The genus *Gastrotheca* encompasses about fifty species known collectively as marsupial frogs. The name literally means "stomach pouch." However, the scientist who named this group overlooked the fact that the pouch in which they rear their eggs and, in some species, their tadpoles, is located on their lower back, not the stomach—although this pouch may curve around to encompass the abdomen. Many early scientists worked with preserved museum specimens only, which are not always in the best condition and certainly far from lifelike. In the case of this group of frogs, it was the presence of eggs and tadpoles in a pouch that involved the sides of the abdomen that undoubtedly led to this erroneous name. When the pouch is closed, it is exceedingly difficult in some species to see the crescent-shaped slitlike opening, especially in preserved specimens.

Marsupial frogs are found in Venezuela to northern Argentina, eastern Brazil and throughout Panama. They are also found on the pacific side of the Andes throughout Colombia and Ecuador. The most commonly available marsupial frogs are *Gastrotheca riobambae* and *G. marsupiata*.

Marsupial Frogs.

Rio Bamba Marsupial Frogs

The Rio Bamba Marsupial Frog is common in gardens throughout large cities in Ecuador, such as Quito, as well as in the surrounding rain forest. Their color patterns are highly variable, but are mainly greens, tans and bronzes in bar shapes or blotches against a lighter tan or beige ground color. Some totally green variants are also seen. It is a chubby little frog reaching lengths of about $2\frac{1}{2}$ to 3 inches and is more terrestrial than most other tree frogs, living among low-lying vegetation near ponds and other bodies of water. It is right at home in large South American cities, existing in public parks as well as private courtyards and gardens, so long as there is a source of water available.

As a high-altitude species, the Rio Bamba prefers temperatures in the 60s to low 70s, and does best in a true aqua-terrarium as it likes to swim. If decorating the cage with substrate, use leaf litter, moss for the land side and provide either a dish (1 to 2 inches deep) of water or a well-filtered partitioned side of water to a height of 4 inches. Also provide rock formations, bark and other natural structures for hiding places. The cage should be well ventilated but need not be heavily humidified.

These frogs are active both during the night and day, and will eat a wide variety of suitably sized insect matter including crickets, mealworms, small moths and flies.

The most fascinating aspect of Rio Bamba Marsupial Frogs is their life history. After the eggs are laid and fertilized by the male, the male assists the female, who uses her hind legs to roll them into the pouch on her lower back where they remain until they become tadpoles or, in some species, fully formed froglets. The female delivers the live young herself, hanging in the water and bending her rear legs backwards, inserting first one foot in the pouch and then the other, stretching it open and allowing either a tadpole to enter the water or a fully formed froglet to emerge. She does this a hundred or more times until every last offspring in her pouch is freed. Marsupial frog tadpoles are vegetarians and will eat boiled lettuce, algae, aquatic plants and vegetarian fish flake food crumbled to a suitable size.

> ## THE MISNOMERS OF SCIENCE
>
> The rules of naming species dictate that the first name given, however erroneous, is the one that sticks. Occasionally, spelling errors may be corrected where proper names are used (as in the case of the American Alligator, which was named after the Mississippi River by a French scientist who misspelled Mississippi!). But even a change such as this requires a formal application to an international commission.

TRUE TREE FROGS

The genus *Hyla* is the largest and most diverse of the tree frog family, with many excellent candidates for both the novice and advanced frog/toad hobbyist. Because there are so many species spread over such a wide part of the world, it is difficult to generalize about them. They are found throughout North, Central and South America, the Caribbean, Eurasia, Europe and northern coastal Africa, north of the Sahara.

Known as the true tree frogs, these species have pads on their toes that enable them to adhere to the sides of trees, walls, aquariums and even tree branches.

Green Tree Frog.

These sticky toe pads are their most distinctive feature. In addition, they have long, slender rear legs enabling them to propel themselves great distances—from branch to branch in fact, in search of a meal, a mate or to escape danger. A number of true tree frogs make excellent cage pets; these are discussed below.

Green Tree Frogs

The Green Tree Frog (*Hyla cinera*) is a U.S. species that is found from the tip of southern New Jersey, south along the Atlantic coastal plain through the Florida Keys, west through the Gulf States to southeastern Texas and north to southern Illinois. There is also an isolated colony in south-central Missouri and this species has been introduced into northwestern Puerto Rico. Because of the bell-like quality of its voice, it is also known as the Bell or Cowbell Frog. It reaches a maximum length of about 2¼ inches. It is usually bright green above with a cream-colored longitudinal "racing stripe" along its sides, although this stripe is very short or nonexistent in some populations.

This frog and its close relatives the Gray Tree Frog (*Hyla versicolor*), Bird Voice Tree Frog (*Hyla avivoca*) and Barking Tree Frog (*Hyla gratiosa*), need a large, tall enclosure that is well-planted with plenty of sturdy branches for them to perch upon. A pool of water should be provided. They eat gut-loaded crickets, mealworms, waxworms, earthworms and winged bugs like small moths and flies. The Barking Tree Frog is the largest native American tree frog, reaching lengths of 2¾ inches, outsized only by the nonnative (introduced) Cuban Tree Frog, the females of which can reach 5 inches in length. These species are readily available in local pet shops or can be collected personally if local regulations permit. They are rarely captive-bred because they are so common and relatively inexpensive. They make excellent "starter" tree frogs, and if well-cared-for, they can live for many years.

Gray Tree Frog.

AUSTRALASIAN TREE FROGS

The genus *Litoria* contains more than 100 different species found in Australia, Australasia, including Papua New Guinea, Indonesia, the Solomon Islands, and Timor. They have also been artificially introduced into New Zealand and New Caledonia. Unquestionably the most readily available and most popular of this group of tree frogs is the White's Tree Frog (*Litoria caerulea*), with second place going to the White-Lipped Tree Frog (*Litoria infrafrenata*). These frogs are sometimes available as wild-caught imports, but their popularity is so great that many frog professionals have been breeding them for years in the U.S. and Europe. Opting for captive-bred, captive-born specimens (although somewhat more costly) means getting a better, healthier and more robust frog that has not had to endure the stress of international air travel or come in loaded with exotic parasites from the wild that would be difficult or impossible to control under captive conditions. More importantly, buying captive-born frogs helps to preserve these species in the wild.

White-Lipped Tree Frog.

White's Tree Frogs

White's Tree Frogs need a terrestrial aquarium that is well-humidified, with the requisite pool or dish of water and a number of sturdy, somewhat larger or broader than usual perches, or better yet, shelves on which to sit. The terrarium should be well-ventilated via a screen cover top. Their preferred temperature range is 65° to 75°F. Given a proper diet and ideal surroundings, these frogs have been known to live for more than twenty years in captivity. Substrate can consist of bark chips or sterile leaf litter or just plain clean, white paper toweling, which should be changed daily. The water also needs to be changed daily. The glass walls of the aquarium should be washed, scraped and cleaned two to three times a week.

These are heavy-bodied frogs, one of a few species of frog that become clinically obese with overfeeding and lack of exercise in captivity. Older specimens develop a fatty flap of tissue above the eyes, which can become so pronounced that it can partially or totally obstruct normal vision. Their color ranges from jade green to bluish-green and all blue specimens are also available. White's Tree Frogs are, however, well-suited to captivity, and they are one of the few exotic species that are recommended to advanced keepers and new-comers alike. They are quite placid and tempting to hold, and will sit still on one's shoulder or hand for varying periods of time. Of course, their behavior is unpredictable and they might hop off at a moment's notice. If they are not in a hurry, this species walks hand-over-hand in a rather slow and deliberate fash-ion—a very endearing trait.

White's Tree Frog.

White's Tree Frogs exude a bitter, toxic, whitish secre-tion to deter predators so it is important to wash your hands thoroughly and immediately after handling them. Females reach 5 inches in length, whereas males reach half that size.

They eat a wide variety of insects, other frogs (includ-ing smaller members of their own species), small snakes, earthworms and newborn mice. Dust food with a multivitamin/mineral powder or gut-load it beforehand. Because of their toxic secretions and penchant for swallowing anything small that moves, it is best to keep only one or a pair of these frogs in a single enclosure. If you keep a pair, make sure the smaller male is at least half the size of the female so she will not be tempted to gobble him up.

*White's Tree Frog
in a blue phase.*

Cuban Tree Frogs

The Cuban Tree Frogs of the genus *Osteopilus* contain three similar species: the Cuban Tree Frog (*Osteopilus septentrionalis*), the Dominican Tree Frog (*Osteopilus dominicensis*) and the Savanna-La-Mar Tree Frog (*Osteopilus brunneus*).

The Cuban Tree Frogs (*Osteopilus septentrionalis*) is the most widely and commonly available in the pet trade in the U.S., and if you happen to live in or visit the southern half of the Florida peninsula you can collect these frogs just about anywhere, with the blessing of the fish and game authorities. Because of Florida's proximity to Cuba, this frog routinely hitches rides on military aircraft and sea vessels as well as private vessels plying the waters between Cuba and Key West, Florida. As a result, it has become a well-established species in most of the southeastern and south-central part of the state. It is now the largest tree frog in the United States, and environmental scientists fear it is crowding out or preying on smaller native species once occupying the niche it now inhabits. They naturally inhabit Cuba, the Bahamas and the Cayman Islands, but have been introduced into Puerto Rico, St. Croix and Hawaii as well as Florida. It is believed that the founder frogs of this species in Hawaii were escaped or deliberately released pets. As they are voracious predators that will even eat hatchling birds in their nests, other frogs and lizards, as well as insects, authorities are worried that this frog could upset the islands' ecological balance. Legislation to prevent further imports of this species onto the Hawaiian Islands, as well as to take measures to control existing stocks, is under consideration.

Cuban Tree Frog.

Cuban Tree Frogs are grayish-white in coloration. Females grow to a length of 5 inches, and males grow to 3 inches. Captives have been known to live more than fifteen years. They have huge toe pads, are extremely agile and are voracious predators of any moving thing that they are able to swallow. They can be found on the walls and doorways of houses at night, gobbling up insects attracted to household lights. During the day they rest. Their preferred activity temperature is in the mid-70s to low-80s. They can withstand short periods of colder temperatures, into the 50s or 60s, but unless they are able to escape such cooler temperatures they do not endure for very long. Part of their success in colonizing Florida and other habitats where they have been introduced is due to their noxious skin secretions, which keep them out of the mouths of predators. Because of their toxic secretions, you should be sure to wash thoroughly after handling them and not to touch your eyes or mouth before doing so.

For captive Cuban Tree Frogs, you will find no shortage of food items. They will eat the usual insect fare and larger females will eat newborn mice.

These frogs are tough and hearty and require a well-planted terrarium with screen cover, a water dish and some sturdy perches or strong broad-leafed plants on which to hang. They should be misted several times a day or placed on an automatic misting system. They are excellent and inexpensive starter species for the new hobbyist.

Spring Peeper calling.

CHORUS FROGS

Spring Peepers

The Spring Peeper (*Pseudacris crucifer*) and some dozen or so related species and subspecies are among the best known frogs to millions of people in the United States even though they have never seen them. They have, however, heard them. Every spring these small frogs begin to chorus or call by the hundreds of thousands, and although invisible to the untrained eye, their voice is well-known as the first sign of spring.

Family Leptodactylidae

These South American tropical frogs include number one on the hit parade of pet frogs: the horned frogs (*Ceratophrys*). Known also as "Pac-Man" frogs because of their large mouth and highly predacious nature, these toads are being captive-bred and sold by the hundreds of thousands every year to frog lovers. They are relatively placid, "sit and wait" predators that stand stock-still most of the time. They are large and colorful. Horned frogs are also capable of biting if you are not careful; they have large, sharp front "snagging" teeth. If they snag you instead of the mouse or other food items you place in front of them, you are apt to get a nasty cut that should be thoroughly washed and disinfected immediately. However, if you are careful not to let these frogs confuse your fingers with their food (using long-handled tongs to feed them small mice is a good idea) you won't get injured.

There are a number of species that can be found in the captive bred pet trade, including albino varieties:

1. *Ceratophrys cranwelli*, known as the Chaco or Cranwell's Horned Frog.
2. *Ceratophrys cornuta*, the Surinam Horned Frog.
3. *Ceratophrys ornata*, the Ornate Horned Frog.

Chaco Horned Frog.

The care and keeping of these and such other members of the genus are basically the same.

Horned frogs should be housed singly because of their predacious nature. Because they are relatively inactive, a single specimen can be comfortably housed in a 5- or 10-gallon covered aquarium. Substrate can consist of either sphagnum moss, bark chips, sterile potting soil or even plain paper toweling. These frogs prefer a warm and humid environment. A water dish should be present and part of the screen cover can be covered with glass to help maintain humidity levels. Their preferred temperatures are between 75° and 85°F; it may be necessary to employ an undertank heating pad in colder weather. The water bowl and tank should be kept clean of any fecal material on a daily basis. Discard and replace substrate every three or four days; paper toweling substrate can easily be changed daily if necessary.

Surinam Horned Frog.

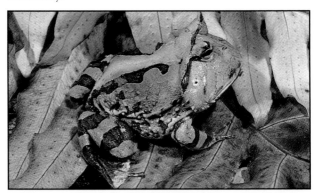

Smaller specimens can be fed a variety of live bugs including mealworms, earthworms, crickets and the like. Larger specimens can be fed newborn mice or rats, graduating to somewhat larger or fuzzy mice or even young "hopper" mice as they grow. To maintain the frogs' color, supplement or gut-load the food you give them with a vitamin/mineral powder. This is particularly important for growing, young frogs that should be fed daily. Adult frogs can be fed every two or three days, although adults of some species will not eat a good-sized meal more than once a week. To avoid getting snagged yourself and to prevent the frog from ingesting any of its substrate (which can cause intestinal obstruction), it is a good idea to offer the frog live food dangling from the end of a long-handled pair of tongs or forceps. You can also help to prevent your frog from getting any intestinal problems by keeping it on a plain white paper toweling substrate.

Ornate Horned Frog.

Family Microhylidae

The Microhylidae or narrow mouthed toads, is a group of about 300 species found throughout the southeastern U.S., west to Texas and lower California, Mexico, and slightly more than half of South America, throughout sub-Saharan Africa, Madagascar, eastern coastal India, Southeast Asia, China and Australasia, including Indonesia and Papua New Guinea.

Sambava Tomato Frog.

Tomato Frogs

The most popular species in the pet trade are the tomato frogs of which there are only three species, all from Madagascar: the Sambava Tomato Frog (*Dyscophus guineti*), the Common Tomato Frog (*Dyscophus anto-gilii*) and the Antsouhy Tomato Frog (*Dyscophus insularis*). These plump, reddish-colored frogs rarely exceed 3 or 4 inches in length. The brightest and largest of the trio is the Common Tomato Frog and is

Antsouhy Tomato Frog.

the species most commonly available as captive-bred in the U.S. In fact, exports from Madagascar have all but ceased due to concerns over dwindling populations, and although the problems faced by these frogs are not all due to the export pet trade, a good percentage of the losses are.

Although wild-caught tomato frogs usually were sold loaded with parasites, which often killed them after a short while in a hobbyist's tank, captive-bred examples are virtually parasite-free and far healthier. These are hearty frogs that accept a wide variety of insects. The largest forms (over 3½ inches) also eat newborn mice. They can withstand a wide range of temperatures, from a low of 50°F to as hot as 90°F, although an optimal range would be in the mid-70s. These frogs need a suitably sized (about one frog per 5 gallons of tank size) aquaterrarium, consisting of both land and shallow water (to a depth of about 3 inches) of equal parts. They require a screen cover and moderate humidity.

Family Pelobatidae

The Pelobatidae family includes the spadefoot toads. There are three genera most commonly obtained as pet frogs:

1. *Pelobates,* consisting of the European Spadefoot Toads (four species) found in Europe, Eurasia and northwestern Africa.

2. *Scaphiopus,* the Eastern (U.S.) Spadefoot Toads, including three species.

3. *Spea,* the Western (U.S.) Spadefoot Toads.

SPADEFOOT TOADS

These are the legendary frogs of the dry plains and deserts, which dig down a meter or more into the substrate, spin themselves a cocoonlike coating of mucoid material to prevent dehydration and remain dormant until the rains come. The Eastern Spadefoot Toad is found east of the Mississippi from Central New England to the Florida Keys and inhabits well-drained sandy habitats.

The Western Spadefoot Toad is found through arid habitats from south-central Canada through central Mexico. These are small, colorful frogs with a specialized protuberance on their rear feet, which they use to shovel their way underground.

*Eastern
Spadefoot Toad.*

These frogs need a terrarium of loosely packed sandy potting soil of 3 to 4 inches in depth. The bottom layers need to be kept damp but the upper layers may be allowed to dry out. This is accomplished by using a 1-inch diameter piece of plastic tubing inserted into the soil just above the bottom layer and then used as a funnel through which you can pour a sufficient amount of water to dampen the bottom layer.

Spadefoot toads are a small species (2 to 3 inches) and require a diet of small insects such as half-grown crickets, mealworms, small earthworms, ants, termites and the like. Spadefoots may be difficult to feed in some situations; this problem, along with their special habitat needs, does not make them a good beginner's frog.

*Western
Spadefoot Toad.*

Family Pipidae

The Pipidae family includes the fully aquatic African Clawed Frogs. This family also contains some seven species of South American aquatic frogs known collectively as Surinam Toads. There are five genera and about thirty species of clawed frogs in all. They are popular aquarium animals, although some species grow large enough to attack and eat tropical fish with which they may be housed. There are several forms of "Dwarf" African Clawed Frogs that do make suitable tankmates for community tropical fish such as guppies, swordtails, mollies and platys.

Dwarf Clawed Frogs

There are five species of Dwarf Clawed Frogs (*Hymenochirus sp.*), all from Africa. These small aquatic species do best in a well-covered, filtered and well-aerated aquarium. Plants, rocks and other hiding places should be provided. Innocuous, small fish species about their same size may be kept with them. These frogs will eat small crickets kicking at the surface, tubifex worms, white worms and other live aquarium foods.

Surinam Toads

The Surinam Toads (*Pipa*) are large, fully aquatic frogs from South America. These frogs are best housed in an aquarium alone. It is possible to keep them with large goldfish or koi; they are guaranteed to swallow any fish that they can. They can be fed feeder tropical fish (but not feeder goldfish), tubifex worms, crickets, mosquitos, other aquatic insect larvae and bait worms. The most frequently available species is *Pipa pipa*. The aquarium should be well-filtered, aerated and covered. A heater is necessary during colder weather and temperatures should be maintained at between 75° and 80°F.

African Clawed Frog.

AFRICAN CLAWED FROGS

The African Clawed Frogs (*Xenopus laevis*) can reach 4 to 5 inches in length. They are fully aquatic and are best kept alone in a well-covered, vigorously filtered and well-aerated aquarium. A heater may be used in winter to maintain water temperature at between 75° and 85°F. These frogs foul their water rather quickly, so one should be prepared to do partial water and filter material changes frequently and complete water changes every seven to ten days. They will eat feeder guppies and other tropical fish, tubifex worms, earthworms and insects that are tossed in the water in their view. Be sure to remove drowned, uneaten insects with a net. These frogs are commercially bred in captivity for laboratory research with some animals diverted to the pet trade.

Family Ranidae

This family has the rather silly name of "True Frogs," which suggests that all the other families of frogs are "false." In any event, these are typical, semiaquatic frogs that structurally resemble one another. This is a very widespread and very large group of frogs with over 700 species in more than fifty genera. They are found throughout North, Central and the northern third of South America, throughout Europe east to China (Eurasia), through sub-Saharan Africa and the Middle East, on the Indian subcontinent east through southern Asia, Indonesia, Papua New Guinea and Australasia. They are absent, except as artificially introduced, in the West Indian and Pacific Oceanic islands.

Most members of the Ranidae family are semiaquatic, but a few species are primarily terrestrial—entering the water periodically to breed, escape enemies, thermoregulate or find food.

POPULAR RANID FROGS

American Bullfrogs

The American Bullfrog (*Rana catesebeiana*) is the largest North American frog species. It gets its name from its call, which sounds like the bellow of a bull. Originally found east of the Rockies, this giant species has spread west to the Pacific coast, where it is preying on and competing with local species. It has been introduced worldwide and can be found in such diverse locations as Italy and other parts of Europe, Cuba, many West Indian islands and Hawaii. It was originally imported into these areas to be farmed as a source of frogs' legs, but has escaped and established itself in the countryside surrounding such open-plan breeding operations.

The American Bullfrog is a semiaquatic species and spends as much or more time in the water as on land. It often remains submerged just below the surface with eyes and nostrils protruding. It needs a large, semiaquatic or aqua-terrarium with significant depth and land to haul out onto. It is a strong jumper, and such enclosures must have a secured screen cover—an unsecured cover could probably be pushed off by this species. The water side needs to be well-filtered and allow for easy water changes, which need to be done frequently.

Male adult bullfrogs can reach lengths of 6 to 7 inches; females are smaller at maximum lengths of 5 inches. This frog is a voracious predator that eats other frogs, including smaller members of its own species; reptiles, including snakes and baby alligators; small mammals; birds and insects. Bullfrogs have even been observed shooting straight out of the water to catch airborne insects such as butterflies, moths or mosquitos. They have also been seen catching and devouring small bats this way. Bullfrogs prefer ingesting and swallowing their prey under water and often submerge before eating prey caught on land or in the air. Preferred temperature ranges from the mid 60s to 70s, although higher and lower temperatures can be tolerated.

American Bullfrog.

Although relatively common and inexpensive, bullfrogs require spacious enclosures or even outdoor ponds to survive long in a captive situation. For this reason, they are not recommended for beginners; there are more interesting, more manageable and smaller ranid species to choose from.

115

Common Leopard Frogs

The Common Leopard Frog (*Rana pipiens*) is a pretty, spotted frog with variable patterns and color combinations, which are dependent on geographic location. It is found throughout North America, but populations of some subspecies are declining. Because this frog is commercially captive-bred for educational and research use, it is relatively inexpensive. This is an active species and is much smaller than the bullfrog—measuring about 3 inches. It requires a semiaquatic aquarium with a strong cover, as these frogs are excellent jumpers. They eat a wide variety of suitably sized insects and make an excellent starter frog. Temperature requirements are in the mid-70s.

*Common
Leopard Frog.*

*Common Wood
Frog.*

Wood Frogs

The Wood Frog (*Rana sylvatica*) is a small species of common terrestrial frog that requires a terrarium with a water dish. It eats small insects, is easy to care for and makes an excellent starter frog for a woodland terrarium with a leaf litter substrate. It tolerates a wide range of temperatures, from as low as 50°F to as high as 80°F. A cover is, of course, required.

Pyxie Bullfrogs

The Pyxie or African Bullfrog (*Pyxicephalus adspersus*) is anything but pixyish. When fully grown, males of this species can reach 10 inches in length, females about 5 to 6 inches. These popular giants are commonly bred in captivity and can be found from mail-order dealers, breeders and occasionally in pet shops. They are a quiet, rather sedentary species that, because of their bulk, can hop rather than jump. Unlike the American Bullfrog, Pyxie Bullfrogs are primarily a terrestrial species and require a terrarium with a suitably sized dish of water for the occasional soak. They spend a majority of their time dug into drier substrates in the wild. In captivity, they should be housed alone in a commodious enclosure. A single full-grown male can be comfortably housed in a 20-gallon aquarium tank. You can use a paper toweling substrate if desired but it would be more at home if it had a soil, bark or litter substrate into which it can burrow. Although it is unlikely that this hefty creature could jump clear out of a tank that is 10 or more inches high, a screen cover is still a good idea. It also prevents your frog from getting any unwanted attention by a family cat or dog. A Pyxie Bullfrog will generally foul its water bowl with every single visit, so the water should be changed whenever this occurs. Its enclosure should be maintained in the 75° to 85°F range.

Pyxie Bullfrog.

These frogs will eat anything that they can swallow, including a wide variety of larger insects such as full-grown crickets, super worms and even mice. Large captives have even been fed small rats and baby chicks.

117

They are cannibalistic and should not be housed with any other frogs, especially smaller ones. Even baby Pyxie Bullfrogs will try to eat their brothers and sisters, so all must be kept in solitary quarters. They also have three sharp teeth on their lower jaw and will not hesitate to bite the hand that feeds them should you come too close; feeding is best accomplished with a pair of long-handled tongs, using techniques similar to those recommended for horned frogs. While frequent handling of any frog is discouraged, Pyxie Bullfrogs can be picked up from around the midriff or you can use an extremely large net or even a birdseed or similar scoop to move or block a frog when you need to do maintenance on its enclosure. Otherwise, these are impressive, hearty and easy to care for frogs that are recommended for the moderately advanced amateur.

Mantella Frogs

Another group of ranids, the frogs of the genus *Mantella,* are colorful, popular and interesting small frogs that reach a maximum length of 1½ inches. These colorful frogs are the equivalent of Madagascar's dart-poison frog, and the island nation of Madagascar is the only place on earth where these unique ranids live. Like dart-poison frogs, they produce a toxic skin secretion which, while not as deadly as that of dart-poison frogs, still dictates the use of the same sorts of handling precautions and considerations recommended previously.

The Mantella frogs are dwindling in numbers and what few examples continue to reach the U.S. are the subject of intense captive breeding programs by professionals so that the hobbyist interest can be sustained without resorting to taking any more of these tiny frogs away from their natural habitat. There are some nine species recognized by science, but scientists are learning new things about this group of animals all the time.

Among the species most commonly seen in the hobbyist or pet trade are: the Golden Mantella (*Mantella aurantica*), an all golden or red-colored frog; the Painted

Mantella (*Mantella madagascarensis*), brightly colored with splotches of lime green, gold, red and even turquoise on a black background; the Fology Mantella (*Mantella laevigata*), which is even more brightly "painted" than the Painted Mantella; and the Green Mantella (*Mantella virdis*), which is mostly lime green with a black mask like a raccoon.

*Golden Mantella
Frogs—all red
(left), all golden
(right).*

It is recommended that you keep Mantellas of the same species together in a single enclosure, but do not keep different Mantella species in one cage. As small but territorial frogs, they need approximately 5 gallons to one frog. A group of four, therefore, could be housed comfortably in a 20-gallon aquarium laid out as a jungle terrarium. It should be well-planted with a waterfall or plastic water dish at one end, with plenty of hiding places such as "caves." Caves can be constructed by using half of a coconut shell, store-bought bark caves over wood, or even the bottoms cut from 2-liter or 1-liter soda bottles. Water bowls should allow these tiny frogs easy access and egress, and should be changed at least daily to prevent build-up of their toxic skin secretions in the water.

Maintain temperatures between 65° and 75°F. Below 65°F they become dormant, and at temperatures above 80°F they become stressed. They are great climbers and jumpers so a secure, tightly fitted screen cover is a necessity. Humidity can be maintained by misting or using an automatic rainmaking device several times a

119

day. Part of the screen cover can be closed with a sheet of plate glass to hold humidity in. A full spectrum fluorescent fixture is also advisable. (It will also help your live plants to grow.) Do not, however, rely on a full aquarium hood as a cover as these small frogs have a way of climbing out into the light fixture or through tiny spaces and escaping. It is preferable, therefore, to place a hood or reflector strip fixture atop a tightly fitted screen cover.

Green Mantella Frog.

Mantella frogs need to be fed daily or at least every second day. These frogs will die without their frequent feedings, so if this schedule will not fit into your lifestyle or if you must travel and do not have an alternate caretaker at home, Mantella frogs are not a good choice. As with the dart-poison frogs, you need to assure a steady, continual source of small live feeder insects including fruit flies, pinhead crickets, ants, termites and the like. Bugs should be lightly dusted with a suitable vitamin/mineral supplement at least once or twice a week.

Properly fed, cared for and housed, these frogs make hearty subjects and are recommended for the advanced amateur with the facilities and commitment to take care of them.

part four

Beyond the Basics

chapter 9

Resources

Books

Bartlett, Patricia P., and Richard D. Bartlett. *Frogs, Toads, and Treefrogs.* Hauppauge, New York: Barrons Educational Series, 1996.

Carpenter, Jill. *Of Frogs and Toads: Poems and Short Prose Featuring Amphibians.* Sewanee, Tennessee: Ione Press, 1998.

Coborn, John. *Frogs and Toads as a New Pet.* Neptune, New Jersey: TFH Publications, 1991.

De Vosjoli, Philippe. *Care and Breeding of Popular Tree Frogs.* Santee, California: Advanced Vivarium Systems, 1997.

Degraaff, Robert M. *The Book of the Toad: A Natural and Magical History of Toad-Human Relations.* Rochester, Vermont: Inner Traditions International Ltd., 1991.

Elliott, Lang, and Cynthia Page. *The Calls of Frogs and Toads.* Buckinghamshire, England: Northwood Audio, 1998 (Book & CD).

Hofrichter, Robert. *The World of Frogs, Toads, Salamanders and Newts.* Ontario, Canada: Firefly Books, 2000.

Morgan, Adrian. *Toads and Toadstools: The Natural History, Folklore, and Cultural Oddities of a Strange Association.* Berkeley, California: Celestial Arts, 1995.

Wright, Albert Hazen, and Roy McDiarmid. *Handbook of Frogs and Toads of the United States and Canada.* Ithaca, New York: Comstock Publishing Association, 1995.

Publications

Reptile and Amphibian Magazine
Box 3709-A, Road 3
Pottsville, PA 17901
(717) 622-6050

Association of Reptile and Amphibian Veterinarians'
(ARAV) Newsletter
To subscribe, contact:
Wilbur Armand, ARAV Executive Director
PO Box 605
Chester, PA 19017

Web Sites

Frogwatch USA
www.mp2-pwrc.usgs.gov/frogwatch

This long term frog and toad monitoring program plans to engage the public in conservation while compiling valuable information about frog and toad populations. Volunteers and scientists can contribute to the Frogwatch USA effort by periodically monitoring a convenient wetland site for the presence of calling frogs and toads. Your findings can be submitted directly to: www.mp2-pwrc.usgs.gov/FrogWatch/index.htm.

Frog Forum
www.frogz.net/netboard

Join this discussion page if you are interested in frogs as pets. A variety of topics—and frogs—are covered, from how to feed a frog while you're away on vacation, where to purchase tadpoles, and ways to identify that odd frog you found in your garden.

The Frog Page
www.geocities.com/TheTropics/1337

Logon to this site to view stylish images of the frog's life cycle, read about how tadpoles develop, and then finish up by jumping on over to look at froggy photographs. This site also provides information and links to other, frog specific pages.

The Somewhat Amusing World of Frogs
www.csu.edu.au/faculty/commerce/account/frogs/frog.htm

If you are interested in finding out everything you can about frogs—and toads—you must visit this Web site. Discover where to find frogs (not in Antartica), how to catch frogs (a process called triangulation works best), and that many frogs are on a continuum between frogs and toads.

The Boreal Toad Homepage
www.mesc.usgs.gov/borealtoad

To find out more about this ancient creature—Boreal toads have been around longer than dinosaurs—logon to this Web site. The United States Geological Survey provides basic information on this toad's alpine and wetlands environment, their endangered status, and what is being done currently to protect them. Also included is an in-depth description of the Boreal toad's life cycle.

The Care and Raising of Oriental Firebellied Toads
http://dencity.com/bombina

If you are interested in these colorful toads which hail from southern China and the Korean peninsula, this is the site for you. Discover in-depth information on Oriental Firebellied Toads, the most popular of all pet toads.

Eggs to Toads
www.monroe2boces.org/shared/esp/eggtoad.htm

For a fascinating look at the life cycle of the common toad, *Bufus americanus*, visit this Web site. Images posted include those of a toad breeding pond, a toad calling, and also follow tadpoles from one to seven weeks of age.

Toad's Dome
www-astro.physics.ox.ac.uk/~erik/toad

From toad poems to toad facts, this Web site has it all. Logon to order a toad tee-shirt, view stunning electronic images of toads, or to simply find out more about toads.

Societies, Organizations and Clubs

To meet a group of like-minded, amphibian-friendly folks, check out the organizations listed below.

American Dendrobatid Group
2932 Sunburst Drive
San Jose, CA 95111
Web: www.xmission.com/~gastown/herpmed/adg.htm
e-mail: powell2@ave.net

International Hylid society
1423 Alabama Street
Lafayette, IN 47905
(317) 742-5331

Society for the Study of Amphibians and Reptiles
(SSAR)
Department of Biology
Saint Louis University
3507 Laclede Street
St. Louis, MO 63103-2010
Web: www.ukans.edu/~ssar
E-mail: ssar@sluvca.slu.edu

Association of Reptilian and Amphibian Veterinarians
(ARAV)
PO Box 1897
Lawrence, KS 66044-88979
www.arav.org/index.html

Live Food (Mail-order and/or Local Pick-up Dealers—U.S. Only) Feeder Insects

Armstrong's Cricket Farm
1127 Wood Street
P.O. Box 125
West Monroe, LA 71924
Inquiries: (318) 387-6000
Cricket Orders Only: (800) 345-8778
Fax: (800) 345-6033
Web: www.armstrongcrickets.com

Grubco
P.O. Box 15001
Hamilton, OH 45015
(800) 222-3563
E-mail: sales@grubco.com
Web: www.grubco.com

Rainbow Mealworms
126 East Spruce Street
Compton, CA 90220
(800) 777-9676
E-mail: order@rainbowmealworms.com
Web: www.rainbowmealworms.com/index.htm

Triple R Cricket Ranch
31585 Road 68
Visalia, CA 93291
(800) 526-4410

Climate and Humidity Control Equipment for Frogs and Toads

Ecologic Technologies
Phone (410) 431-7106
E-mail: mistingkits@cs.com,mistingsystems@
cloudtops.com
Web: www.cloudtops.com

Ecologic Technologies supplies rainmaking and automated misting equipment.

Helix Controls
914 Santa Fe Avenue
Vista, CA 92054
(760) 726-4464
E-mail: support@helixcontrols.com
Web: http://helixcontrols.com

Contact Helix for thermostatic heating control
supplies.